Quality of Life

D1488123

Quality of Life

Life

5 Stages of Retirement Success

Karen Bachert

Quality of Life

Requests for information should be addressed to:

Evangel Press

2000 Evangel Way

P.O. Box 189

Nappanee, Indiana 46550

prepress@evangelpress.com

Cover design by Matthew R. Gable

About the Cover

An icon of enthusiasm, optimism, and new beginnings, the coral rose is the symbol of our lives and our future. The cover photo, taken in the beautiful rose garden at the author's home, was photographed by her husband, Ray Bachert—who is also their gardener.

Edited by Kathy L. Borsa

ISBN-13: 978-0-9818789-0-4

ISBN-10: 0-9818789-0-3

Library of Congress Control Number: 2008906707

Printed in the United States of America

1 2 3 4 5 EP 12 11 10 09 08

Dedication

With sincere gratitude, I express my appreciation to all who have contributed to the creation of *Quality of Life,* and I dedicate this effort:

To my parents, who were the first people in my life to love me unconditionally and to instill in me the courage to try.

To my husband Ray, who gives me his confidence and encouragement in everything I do.

To those who read my manuscript and gave me feedback—my daughters Shelly, Susie, and Mary; my friend Christine; my mom; and my editor Kathy.

To those who shared their retirement insights and contributed to the content of the book, especially Barb, Joetta, Patti and Dick, Don and Barb, my mom, Ray's mom, and Aunt Ruthie.

To those who first endorsed this project—Traci, Kim, Nouli, Rosanna, Amy, and Dr. Henderson.

To Roger Williams, who gave me guidance, and to all the development team at Evangel Press—thank you for your talents and enthusiasm.

To our daughters and their husbands, who remind me that with God's help, we can make this world a better place.

To Lynn and John, who have shared our life and been our very best friends for more than forty years.

To my grandma, who left me her legacy of faith, hope, and unconditional love.

To our grandchildren, who we love with all our hearts: Ally, Carrie, Katie, and Annie; Mike, Max, and Miles; and Lucy, Luke, and Eli.

Endorsements

"She will help her readers and audiences to find the path to their own success, to look forward with an optimistic view of life, and to enjoy every moment of life."

Despina Platia, Athens, Greece
International Marketing and P.R. Specialist

"I believe that, in my life, I will never again come across a person with such ability to transmit enthusiasm, empathy, and so professionally skilled at conveying messages. . . . An energy giver."

Rosanna Cassamassima, Rimini, Italy
International Export and Marketing Consultant

Message to My Readers

It is my pleasure to introduce myself and to share a little bit about my life with you. I am a wife, mother, grandmother, and daughter. I am also an entrepreneur, a conference host, a motivational speaker, a writer, and a mentor.

After thirty years in Corporate America I retired and after enjoying a prosperous, meaningful career life that gave me the opportunity to touch the lives of hundreds of people and to help them discover their own potential and to realize their own future. My husband and I spent a number of years commuting back and forth from our home in South Bend, Indiana, to Milan, Italy, and to Athens, Greece, where I enjoyed the opportunity to work with some wonderful people and to experience new cultures and new business opportunities.

My personal mission includes motivation, inspiration, and a deep desire to express myself in ways that help others discover themselves. I want to motivate, to inspire, and to guide other people through my writing, my seminars, and through my individual coaching to help them discover themselves and to strive to be the best they can be.

I want to create and to maintain a balance in life that supports a successful retirement that includes family, leisure, self-expression, and personal contribution. I want to make a difference in the lives of other people.

Through the launching of my first book, *Quality of Life: The Five Stages of Retirement Success,* I want to help you to discover your best self. Through the depth of my own experiences and the experiences of others who have shared so generously of themselves, I invite you to walk with me from preretirement planning, to the first year of discovery, to moving forward, to living our lives to the fullest, to leaving a legacy.

I sincerely hope you will enjoy reading *Quality Of Life* and that in some small way you will be inspired as you join me in our journey into our future. Please know that I have thought of you often as I wrote this book, and I have even imagined who you are and whom you will become. Just as the experience of writing this book has inspired me, I hope to inspire you. Together we can explore and discover, we can choose to wander off life's everyday path, and each of us can become the person God intended us to be.

Contact me to make arrangements for a conference or speaking engagement for your group or to request copies of my book. I'd love to hear from you.

With warmest regards,

Karen Bachert, K Enterprises
574-344-8895

To e-mail Karen—karenkenterprises@sbcglobal.net
To order books—bookskenterprises@sbcglobal.net

Table of Contents

Introduction

It will soon be one year since I retired. My career life which encompassed more than thirty years of rewarding and interesting challenges and opportunities came to an end allowing a new beginning in what I like to call "the adventures of early retirement." I'm settling in to find my place and I'm starting the project of discovering my new beginning. I hope to help you find your place too, and I invite you to begin your journey with me. A new and exciting life awaits us.

My personal mission includes motivation, inspiration, and a deep desire to express myself in ways that can help others discover themselves. I want to take time to lend a hand and be kind and considerate of others. I know the value of doing what makes you feel good about yourself. I find inspiration in the words of Harry Emerson Fosdick, "Doing what makes you feel good about yourself is not self-indulgence. It's not gratifying an isolated part of you but satisfying the whole you and that includes the feelings and ties and responsibilities you have to other people."

Let life begin at thirty, or fifty, or seventy or whenever we are so moved to make a change in ourselves or decide to make a difference in the lives of others. For me at fifty-eight, the thought of retiring was very inviting—something I had always anticipated I would do earlier than others might expect. Undoubtedly, I am a firm believer that everyone should exit the workplace into retirement gracefully and eagerly with certainty that we will find pleasure and fulfillment in this exciting, new stage of our lives.

And yet, when the time actually came, I was more than a little apprehensive. I must admit, occasionally my certainty was mixed with shades of doubt. Sometimes, just for a few fleeting moments, a sense of loss and uneasiness invaded my positive, enthusiastic self. What happens to our identity? What happens to who we are and who we have been? What's next in life's journey?

When all was said and done, the "Saying good-bye to yesterday," really wasn't all that hard for me. I was ready. It was part of my plan. The rewards of my career were meaningful and will certainly be valuable to my future, but just like so many others I have talked to and interviewed, it is surprising how, even though we may have some doubts, we tend to rather quickly realize we really are ready to move on.

I was lucky in the fact that I moved forward surrounded with support and encouragement from my family. My husband Ray had retired a few years earlier and we both had enjoyed the opportunity to travel frequently to Europe together during those last few years. I was traveling on business, and he was traveling with me. That gave us the opportunity to share this experience—one we will both treasure as an opportunity few couples really have in life.

As I approached readiness for making my retirement announcement, Ray gave me his calm and confident reassurance and tried to help me make light of this transition. After all, it wasn't really like us to always have *all* our ducks in a row. "It's all going to work out," he would remind me with his relaxed, self-assurance and understated manner that he uses when I am in doubt or over-extending my tendency to worry.

My three daughters, one-by-one, pushed a little to help me get ready. It was time. It was the right thing to do. "Go ahead and just do it!"

I looked back on my career life journey. Starting out as a part-time customer service representative, I had worked hard to climb the corporate ladder, one promotion at a time, to become the senior vice president of my company. And, for the most part, I knew that I had thrived on the chaotic pace of Corporate America. Yet, at the same time, I also knew that I was ready to move on.

I was ready to announce my plans to retire. I'll tell you just a few more things that I think will help to illustrate some of the turmoil that becomes part of this preretirement-stage adjustment period.

I knew that with our six grandchildren and the two more who would arrive very soon, my work life was far too consuming to allow me the time and energy to really enjoy watching them grow. I wanted to be a meaningful part of each of their lives. My beautiful and wonderful daughters, strong and independent, had everything under control, and I didn't really need to help them with their families or even be on hand on any regular basis, but I was determined to not let those years slip away and miss out on all the fun of little grandchildren.

Mary, our youngest daughter, who had a history of premature births with her first two boys, was now on bed rest working hard to put in the "down time" required to give her new baby the best start in life possible. It's not an easy task for anyone, but for Mary with three-year-old, super-energetic Max and four-year-old Michael, who challenges the best of us to stay two steps ahead of him, it was even more demanding. She could use my help now, and I really wanted to be with her and support her. My thoughts processed the reality.

There was still another nudge to help me along the way. Shelly, our oldest daughter and a nurse, seemed to be more aware of how the pressures of my work were affecting me. I remember how shocked I was when she gently warned me, "Mom, I'm afraid that if you continue at this pace you'll cut your own life short." She really meant it and in her firm, tell-it-like-it-is way, cautioned me to think about the fact that stress can actually cut your life short.

She put it in perspective for me when she said it could mean the difference between adding or subtracting five extra years to or from my life. Oh, I am not so sure Shelly's concerns were as real as she thought, but clearly she reminded me how much I was loved by my family. I knew they really wanted more of me in their lives and retiring would give me the opportunity to embrace this wonderful adult relationship with my daughters in a new and very meaningful way.

Yes, decisions need to be made and directions need to be chosen, but even after we make the move and announce our retirement we don't have to rush right into our new life. In fact, for most of us it is good to pause to think and take a few baby steps into self-discovery before we make too many decisions or set our directions too firmly in place for our future. Let's explore as we take time to enjoy the journey along the way.

Our *Stage One* will be *Preretirement Preparation*. It's the anticipation and planning stage. We'll transform a dream into a plan and learn from others who have experienced the journey or have expertise to guide us in our process.

Stage Two will be focused on the first year after we formally move into retirement. It's the first year—the year of exploration. We'll learn more about the benefits of *Reading, Relaxing, Refreshing, and Refocusing*. It'll be like the first year of employment as an executive in a new company. We must expect ourselves to contribute to the success of our lives in retirement from day one, but at the same time, we need to get to know life's players better and truly understand the direction and purpose of our lives. What is it that our Creator expects from us during this stage of our life? How do we understand the process of discovery that prepares us to move forward with the rest of our lives?

During *Stage Three* we'll be *Moving Forward*. For the most part, we will know where we are going, and our day-to-day lives will always have meaning and purpose. Each day will be new. Many challenges, although anticipated, will startle us at first and require the support and encouragement of our loved ones and friends. We will be grounded in our identity and committed to giving of ourselves to those around us.

Stage Four will be about living our lives to their fullest, with no regrets. Just *Live Life*. Every day will be cemented with unconditional love that we will try to freely give to those around us. Learning will continue to be our passion and discovering, our enthusiasm. Self-centeredness will give way to giving of ourselves to the things we really value in life with real care and compassion. We will become the person we want to be.

Stage Five, Leaving a Legacy. Life is good and we appreciate the wonders of the world around us. We know that some day we will be ready to move on to God's kingdom. We'll be ready for a new beginning, a new adventure, and we'll leave behind a legacy of hope, faith, and encouragement that will give others the courage they need to move forward adding new meaning and purpose to their lives.

This won't happen right away. At least that's not our plan, but when it does we'll be ready, and we will have done our best to prepare those we love. We'll continue to celebrate our retirement. Our retirement life will be all that we want it to be!

Stage One

Preretirement Preparation

It seems this phase begins somewhere between age forty-five and sixty. I'm not talking just about the investment representative's view of promoting a life savings plan that prepares us financially for retirement. There is more to it than money, although that certainly is an important subject we all need to delve into. On the subject of money, I'll simply begin by saying, "The earlier you start saving for your retirement the better." The financial stress of planning your retirement can be overwhelming, and everyone needs to take that message seriously.

However, many of us are from a pampered generation. We've never really had to do without. So, therefore, we can easily fall into complacency about retirement planning and financial security allowing ourselves to stay caught up in the here and now. Kids, college fees, weddings, and day-to-day living leave us neglecting the need to discipline ourselves to save for retirement. We neglect to follow a plan that will produce the results that we want to support the retirement we'll dream about someday.

It is too bad that even the idea of dreaming about retirement seems to be something we postpone and sometimes even dread. I don't mean the "stopping work" part. I think most people do look forward to leaving employment life, but too many people worry that the other side of retirement may not be much more than a sure sign of getting older.

I apologize for using such a cliché, but I am afraid it's true—we'll probably only end up feeling as old as we allow ourselves to feel. However, the need to finance our retirement is a reality. And how well we finance it can actually play a big part in how young or how old we feel during our retirement years. It's not all about money, but it is about planning and preparing and making some good decisions along the way.

A financial planner or investment advisor, a continuing education class at a local college, and the words and wisdom of parents who have done well in creating their own plan can help us. However, it is really important that we recognize the statistics that tell us early retirement (for most between sixty and sixty-two) will be a reality for most of us. Changing things, changes in us, work situations, and health issues all influence our decision and our direction. Retirement often comes at least a few years earlier than most people have planned for it.

Preretirement planning allows us time to contemplate and to openly discuss our options with our spouse and our family. To get ourselves financially, mentally, and emotionally ready, here are some things to consider.

Chapter 1

Timing

It is a good idea to make sure you are ready to retire before you announce your plans to your boss, your staff, or coworkers. You want your retirement announcement to be made on your terms, not on your boss's, so be sure to keep your announcement strictly confidential until your retirement plan is clearly in place.

You need a target date for your retirement and a contingency plan for an immediate exit if your plan-for-retirement announcement is met with resistance. Your boss may ignore your intentions and continue business as usual or react—pushing you forward to retirement sooner than you planned.

For some, part-time employment may be an important financial component of retirement or early retirement. Just be aware, you may or may not be able to negotiate part-time employment with your current employer. If you have been in a high-profile position and you failed to negotiate a retirement package years ago, your employer may simply respond to your plans to retire by thanking you for your years of service and wishing you well as you move into retirement.

After all, it is hard to move forward in a company when an executive who has retired from a high level position stays around as a part-time consultant. It is also difficult for top-level executives to step down to consultancy. For me, breaking the ties after thirty years allowed me the freedom to explore my new future and enjoy the pleasures of early retirement. It is a good feeling to know you really can put your work days behind you.

A Lesson From My Parents

My parents gave us a great life lesson about retirement and ending their career life early. My father was self-employed, a real self-made man, who built his own business and supported his family. By financial measurements he was quite successful and was able to retire in his mid-fifties. He and my mom had a great retirement, enjoyed golfing and "snow birding" back and forth between their mid western, small-town life and their golf course resort home just north of Orlando.

Dad died a few months before his seventieth birthday. It was far sooner than any of us anticipated, but I am so glad he truly enjoyed the opportunity early retirement gave him to spend time with his family. Grandkids visited them in Florida during every spring break. Summers were spent following the grandkids from one sporting event to another. For Dad and Mom, this was a real extension of their earlier married years when their own children played sports and went on family picnics and fishing trips. Dad left us a treasure of memories we will always carry with us.

Yes, his career was very important to him, and we were all very proud of his accomplishments but, interestingly enough, when the priest asked us (his six children) to write his eulogy, each of us gave our input and our memories of our relationship with Dad and yet none of us elaborated on his business success. We were all very proud of his business success—I guess that goes without saying, but to his family, he was someone we truly knew and loved. He made an enormous impact on each of our lives that we will all always cherish.

I tell this story to remind myself that, although saying good-bye to our work life may have some moments of apprehension and some fear of losing some part of our identity, I really think our identity influences our work but our work does not mold our identity. It only gives us another avenue to express ourselves and to, hopefully, make a difference in the world we live in.

This preretirement stage is certainly an important stage, and I sincerely hope that each of you will have the opportunity to think more about your life and the things that are really important to you. How will your plans for retirement help you to become the person you always wanted to be?

Even if you plan to work part-time during your early retirement years, I suggest your preretirement planning allows six months to one year of financial stability after you retire, without the need for a paycheck. If you can swing it financially, you will want to take the time to ponder and explore for a while before you add part-time employment to your retirement life.

Chapter 2

Create and Manage Your Personal Financial Situation

Preretirement requires an honest attempt at gaining an in-depth understanding of your long-term financial needs. Investments, taxes, social security, health insurance, long-term care insurance, and life insurance are just some of the topics of interest and necessity. Don't delegate the responsibilities of your financial future to anyone else. Find an investment representative and/or a financial advisor whom you trust. Create an investment strategy and follow its process. Ask questions, research, follow, and monitor the process.

Our financial advisor recently told me a story of a woman's reaction to a seminar he was conducting on financial planning for women. When doing follow-up calls to confirm attendance at his seminar, the financial advisor asked the woman if she planned to attend the seminar. Her response was "No, I'm really not into playing the money game. I leave the financial stuff to my husband." Huge mistake! The vast majority of married women outlive their husbands and need to understand that their life expectancy dictates that women will assume full responsibility for finances at some point in their future. We can't ignore it. It is necessary to get involved in finances and prepare to handle our money and our future.

How do we know if our nest egg is big enough to retire? There are many retirement planning tools available through investment representatives, financial advisors, and even the Internet that can give you a good idea about how far your nest egg will take you. However, it all starts with your own understanding of your lifestyle needs and the annual income you will need to support your retirement.

Some experts suggest that 75% to 80% of your current annual salary is a rough estimate of how much money we will need in retirement each year. Your planning tools will help you project your anticipated earnings on your investments and will factor in inflation.

However, you have got to start with a good idea of how much money you plan to live on annually in retirement. I suggest that it may also be a good idea to look at your income during the last five years and your savings plan during that period. For my husband and me, we were saving 20% of our income during those last five years and that made a big difference when calculating our retirement needs. We were already quite used to living on 80% of our income and our retirement plan took us comfortably down to living on less than 60% of our income during our first years of retirement.

You May Be Able to Retire Earlier Than You Think

This was a very positive discovery and I hope you will find some very positive and encouraging information that will help you to be able to anticipate your retirement, or even semiretirement, earlier than you might think. If it is important to you to retire early, you can do well by investigating the possibilities thoroughly to determine how much money you will need and where it might come from.

There are lots of things to consider including how your lifestyle will change during retirement and how those changes will affect your budget. Therefore, it is good to work with real numbers and get some financial expert assistance to create your financial plan for retirement. A good plan in the early stages of retirement planning will help us feel secure for the long haul and allow us the freedom to explore and discover our new beginning.

Don't be afraid of retirement and don't delay it for old age either. Retirement offers enormous opportunities for happiness, fulfillment, and living a life of meaning and purpose. Every day counts. Go after your retirement! Dream and believe with energy and enthusiasm!

Chapter 3

Define Your Priorities

Married Couples Come Together and Define Your Future

Married couples need to come together on the subject and make financial planning an important part of planning their future together. Retirement is meant to be a time for married couples to join forces like never before and to share their future—their day-to-day lifestyle, entertainment and travel, purpose and productivity, money and money management, spirituality and self-expression. These are all subjects we need to discuss and to explore. Not only from a financial standpoint but, for the meaning and purpose of the rest of our married lives together, we need to join forces in our thinking and in our values.

What is really important to you? What is really important to your spouse? I suggest every couple and every individual contemplating retirement sit down and write a retirement plan that defines your desired retirement life.

Please reflect on the following topics and then on page 87 of the Appendix, I will share messages from others who either have already embarked on retirement or are in the process. Then, on page 93, I will ask you to respond to these topics yourself. I hope their stories will help you shed light on your own plan. I'll continue to encourage you to take time to sort things out but to avoid procrastinating too long. *The joys of retirement await you*!

Make the decision to retire

Your first year of retirement

Financial security and lifestyle satisfaction

Travel and activities

Together and individual interests

Leisure time

Day-to-day living

Family

Money

Someday dreams

Self-expression

Volunteering

Part-time employment

Spirituality

Purpose in life

Health and fitness

Chronic illness, disease, and physical limitations

Words of wisdom

Growing old together/growing old alone

Advice for others who are retiring

Chapter 4

Develop a Positive Attitude and Outlook

Your retirement will be what you want it to be and what you make of it. Retirement success and retirement happiness depend on our ability to react to the opportunities that will present themselves to us in the days and weeks ahead when getting up every day and going to work is no longer the necessity.

Many people believe they know what they will do when they retire. They'll pursue their favorite hobbies, spend time with grandkids, or travel. They'll entertain more or do some volunteer work. They'll relax, read, and slow down and smell the roses.

And, sharing in my own good fortune, I hope they'll be able to spend quality time with parents and loved ones. After all, time spent gathering Mom's memories and marveling at Dad's wisdom will be time spent wisely and wonderfully.

And, if we are lucky enough and wise enough to value our good fortune, some of us will be able to get to know our children and our friends and our spouses in a new way and develop a relationship that goes beyond loving and caring for and becomes life's most valuable treasures forever. We'll intertwine all those precious opportunities, and they will influence who we are and how we influence others too.

Oh my goodness, let's not dread getting older and worry about boredom or loneliness. True meaning and fulfillment for each of us in our retirement years begin with a positive attitude and an outlook that anticipates and creates a future that is uniquely our own. Oh, there is so much to do, be, learn, see, and think about. We have the maturity and the insight to know every day is an opportunity ready to be captured.

With the Gift of His Love

We can be and continue to become the person God truly intended us to be. We can commit ourselves to worry or boredom or to enthusiasm and discovery. Our commitment can be to live our lives every day to their fullest and make the world a better place for ourselves and for others. Our attitude is our own creation and, like it or not, it will pass on to generations to come. God didn't make any mistakes. The gift of His love and the privilege to share it with others belongs to all of us. It begins with an attitude—an optimistic attitude. It is supported by an outlook that anticipates good things and a determination to influence the world around us in a positive way.

Preretirement is time to remind ourselves of our own personal core values and remember who we are and who we want to be. It is time to give our lives the meaning often lost in our commercialized surroundings and in the stress of day-to-day living. I share with you a little prayer found when I was cleaning out my desk anticipating retirement. In retirement I'll really try to do a better job at this.

Oh Lord, grant that each one who has to do with me today may be happier for it. Let it be given me each hour today what I shall say, and grant me the wisdom of a loving heart that I may say the right things rightly. Help me to enter into the minds of everyone who talks with me, and keep me alive to the feelings of each one present. Give me a quick eye for the little kindnesses that I may be ready in doing them and gracious in receiving them. Give me a quick perception of the feelings and needs of others and make me eager hearted in helping them. Amen.

(Author Unknown)

Chapter 5

Just Do It!

Now It Is Time to Make Your Retirement Announcement.

Once you've got your plan in order and you feel pretty secure in your decision, don't procrastinate. Just do it and do it with integrity and dignity. Make your retirement announcement following the format of your company.

Hopefully, we'll each leave our workplace feeling quite appreciated at least by some. We'll take with us the knowledge we have helped others who crossed our path, and we'll plan to keep in touch with those we spent so much time with each day.

Give generously without expecting anything in return to those who follow you. If you have the opportunity to mentor and contribute to your transition, do it. Don't hold back, even if you know some may quickly discount the value of your experience. You'll be happier for it.

We all know people who have left their jobs spiteful and full of resentment. They have somehow tried to make everyone miserable and uncomfortable as they leave their companies. We've been there and have all witnessed that disaster. Therefore, I'm going to forgo the need to paint the picture and tell the story with an example.

Hindsight suggests it is usually about someone who doesn't feel appreciated. The fact is that I tend to believe that probably few people really feel adequately appreciated for their years of service to their company when they retire. Human nature prompts us all to value being appreciated, and countless leadership training programs tell us that not feeling appreciated is really a big deal for most employees. But if it happens when we retire, and we know that it most likely will (at least to some degree), let's decide to let it go.

Let's focus on anticipating the good stuff. I suspect all of us will be pleasantly surprised by the thoughtfulness of some of the people we work with and for. Let's enjoy these expressions of appreciation and recognition for what they are, genuine expressions of good wishes. Some will sincerely appreciate our help and contributions and some will not. Most importantly, we'll know we have done a good job.

Good-bye to the workdays of yesterday, and hello to all of our tomorrows.

Stage Two

The First Year of Retirement

This is when I really knew the value of a clean break. It felt so good—so free. I flirted with the idea of part-time consultancy, but gladly that didn't materialize. I retired. I was finished with my job and ready to take my first steps at discovering my future. During this chapter we're going to talk about creating a new balance in our lives—about exploring and about self-identity. We begin the day we retire, and the process will likely last about a year.

Barb, a good friend of mine and a colleague for many years, retired three or four years ahead of me. We kind of lost touch after she retired, but she was one of the first people I was drawn to contact soon after retirement. I called Barb and asked her to join me for lunch. I hadn't seen her in a while and Barb looked great. She blossomed with enthusiasm about life, and in her very unpretentious, light-hearted way, she encouraged me to take time to figure out what I was going to do with myself. I told her that I didn't really know what I was going to do now that I had retired. It was kind of an embarrassment to actually tell her that, but it was the truth and that is where I really was at that moment.

I didn't have a clue as to what I planned to do with my retirement. She shared a little bit of her own experience, "First I cleaned my house from top to bottom and while I was cleaning I began the process of figuring out what I wanted to do." Barb encouraged me to "take my time" and reassured me that I'd "figure it out." I guess she already knew that this part of retirement was a process, and she was quite content with the fact that it all works out, and we all really do decide what we are going to do next.

Have Fun and Be Adventuresome

Her words were brief and simple but her tone told me to trust her message. I think that was really the first time I realized that I was starting a process to really understand what I wanted to do with the rest of my life. Few of us really walk into retirement with a clear understanding of where we are headed and how we will get there. As my friend Barb encouraged me, I encourage you. Your first year of retirement has time for exploration. Have fun with it and be adventuresome. And if I may be so bold as to predict, I think you will be pleasantly surprised where your adventure may take you. I am eager to share my process with you.

Chapter 6

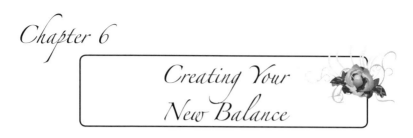

Creating Your New Balance

Before we begin to explore and find ourselves lost in the process of the challenging adventure, we need to create a new balance in our lives. The business of organizing ourselves and putting our house in order needs to be tended to. We live in a different world now and, if we are married, share it with our spouse. If we are not married, we still need to consider all the people who are currently in our lives and anticipate some new faces who will undoubtedly become a more involved part of our future. After all, retirement means less time at work and more time to spend doing other things, and we will need to adjust our relationships with other people in our lives to accommodate the transition. We'll need to reorganize our day-to-day activities to fit our needs and the needs of others.

Retirement Needs Space to Grow and Develop

Reorganize as you see fit. Most of us do plan more time to enjoy our homes or to begin to dream about a new home that will support our new lifestyle. However, since this stage of retirement is about exploring and discovering, I do encourage you to delay moving to a new city or new home for one year. Let's avoid the temptation to jump from the busyness of our work life and create the same busyness model in retirement. Retirement is meant to be the time that we can become the best we can be. The enriching, rewarding, retirement model most of us want needs to be created. It needs space to grow and develop.

Our first year needs a little structure that comes from creating a balance. Some need routine, an exercise class, some volunteer work, a hobby, a mission, or a project. Others need time for travel, if they are so inclined, and some need time to rekindle special relationships with long-lost friends. Retirees and soon-to-be-retirees unite. It is a great time to talk to those who are doing retirement right and separate ourselves from those who aren't.

After all, we already decided that retirement will be an exciting adventure. We've chosen our attitude and outlook, and we don't want to clutter things up by making too many decisions too quickly. Now there's time to do the things we want to do. The big question is: What are the things we always thought we wanted to do and do we still want to do them?

I think that many of us are in for some big surprises. Some of the things we thought we'd always want to do aren't really that inviting. We've changed as we've matured. On the same token, some of the things we thought we'd never like to do become interesting and enticing when the freedom of retirement gives us a different outlook and the opportunity to explore. One step leads to another and another and another.

We're ready and we can have a lot of fun during this first year and do well by just letting ourselves wander a bit into our new world of self-discovery.

Chapter 7

Reading, Relaxing, Refreshing, and Refocusing

Here is a simple way to guide our transition. The "four "R's" are reading, relaxing, refreshing, and refocusing. They are easy to remember and meaningful in their content. I suggest you can explore one topic at a time or bounce from one to another. We just need to remember to stay connected to the process. The process is the launching pad for our future.

I retired on May 23, 2006, and my journey needed to allow me to travel in self-discovery for one full year. I explored so many subjects. I contemplated and hesitated but continued to move in the right direction to create the retirement package I wanted to own and to live with the rest of my life. I'll share my discoveries along the way as I invite you, once again, to travel with me.

It is a new beginning but very different from all of our new beginnings before. It's distinctly unique, different than when we got married, or when the kids went off to college or when they got married or even when the first grandchild was born. This new beginning carries with it our maturity, our wisdom, and our power for self-discovery. I remember contemplating my journey and reminding myself that my future could be thirty years or forty years or more. Or, my future could be only a moment. Those are the things we can't determine, but I knew that my future was mine to claim and to shape into my own. Your future is yours too, and I encourage you to claim it and shape it into the life you want it to be.

Reading—Spiritual, Intellectual, and Inspirational

Our reading habits during our self-discovery year will contribute to the fulfillment and satisfaction of our retirement life. Our libraries and our book stores are filled with an abundance of treasures that will give us encouragement and inspiration as we explore our own unique, individual opportunities. Take time to browse among the shelves and surf the Internet pages. What are your hidden talents and interests? Dabble in an art class; take a course at your local college. Enjoy your adventure. Search for wisdom. The world around us will soon begin to put new value on our life experiences and look to us for insight.

I never really had a passion for reading before my retirement. I guess my life was just so complicated and demanding that I didn't think there was time to read much. So if you have always enjoyed reading or if you just finally find time to get lost in the pages of a good book, I encourage you to read. We enrich our lives, enhance our minds, and find our future in the pages of inspiration. Self-discovery gives way to self-development and a lifetime of learning that inspires our destiny.

The best way to learn is to teach, as we discover and learn we have a responsibility to share the experience with others. How can I enrich the life of someone else? Whose life can be touched by sharing my newly found insight and wisdom? If we are so lucky, we have a grandchild—a six-year-old or a sixteen-year-old. Or we may have a daughter or son who is a newlywed or a new mom or dad. A lonely neighbor, a homebound friend, or an octogenarian can also share our discoveries with us.

Seeing Things Through Mom's Eyes

During my first year of retirement, my mom had some medical challenges that prompted me to spend more time with her—quiet time, just talking, as she recuperated. I'm delighted I had this wonderful opportunity. My treasure chest is filled up with hours of seeing things through Mom's eyes. I marvel at her wisdom and insight and her unbelievable ability to genuinely tune in to other people and describe their behavior with a deep understanding of who they are and what makes them tick. Oh, if some day I could understand my own children and grandchildren to the depth my mom understands her six children, sixteen grandchildren, and twenty great-grandchildren. As I author my first book, my mom is my greatest encourager and most valued critic.

The moral of my story is this: Read, explore, learn, and share the experience with a six-year-old, a sixteen-year-old, your son or daughter, and an eighty-year-old. When you give of yourself, you'll feel valued and appreciated. Gather treasures that will inspire and motivate your future, and you will give value to every day for the rest of your life.

Read and learn and learn and teach. Choose a mix of spiritual, intellectual, and inspirational topics. From the pages of your book and the insight of your experience to the depths of your heart, you will begin to unlock your treasures. Delight in the rewards of sharing yourself with others.

Relax—Take Time to Smell the Roses

Don't get me wrong, retirement life can easily become quite hectic and demanding. As we discussed earlier in this chapter, there needs to be a balance. We can't let ourselves switch from working life busyness to retirement busyness. We have to avoid the clutter to create the freedom. There needs to be time to relax and enjoy the pleasures of the opportunity. Our vacation time is no longer limited to two or three weeks at best each year.

We can travel and take time to enjoy our journey and dare to dart off the chosen path and explore. We have the opportunity to linger to learn more and marvel at God's creations—the sunset, the sunrise, the mountains, the seas, and the skies. We can fish, ski, golf, go bicycling, or just go for a walk—or plan and take a trip. There's time to enjoy the company of old friends and even time to get to know new ones. We can share our interests and find new interests. As we take time to relax and enjoy the wonders of the world and the wonders of our life, old habits can be broken and new ones acquired.

The things that we do need to become more than just things to do. For me, I thoroughly appreciate anticipation in everything that I plan to do. Spontaneity surely has its place in my life, but the fun of anticipating an outing, a party, travel, or a visit from old friends is really half the fun. I like having fun things to do on my calendar and having the freedom of a lifestyle that allows me to wander and linger and recharge. Life is full of inspiration and my inspiration comes when I am knee-deep in activities that relax my body and recharge my soul.

Refresh—The Secret Ingredient in the Fountain of Fulfillment

We all know them—people in our lives who seem to have endless energy and exuberance. Always on top of their game and seeming to never wear down, they are and will always be young at heart, young in mind, and young in spirit. They're not hyper or overly excitable but genuine, available, and real. Their secret is hidden in the fact that, along life's journey, they have learned how to refresh.

I have somehow tuned into their magic at this late stage of my life, not because I practice the art of refreshing so skillfully myself, but more in the light of admiration. Those who know how to refresh their body, their mind, and their soul truly have discovered their own fountain of fulfillment. Regular exercise (the kind that is fun), good nutrition, and restful sleep habits seem to play a big part in this refreshment process.

I encourage all of us to make a real effort to keep regular exercise a part of our lives. It is my challenge to us to eat healthier and, if we have extra pounds, to put the brakes on overindulgence. And adapting good sleep habits will also benefit us greatly. If we have any bad habits that we know will limit the quality of our lives like smoking or excessive use of alcohol, we need to tackle these issues and refresh our bodies.

Mental habits that need adjustments may have to do with worrying too much, especially about things that we can do little about. Judgmental or gossipy, self-centeredness tends to support the idea we may think more highly of ourselves than of others. Self-criticism leaves us with scars created by guilt and supported by a habit of kicking ourselves when we are down. Let's get over it and refresh who we are with a new attitude that is more accepting of the limitations of others and less critical of ourselves and the world around us.

Again, I certainly don't claim to have all the answers on this subject, but motivational and inspirational reading helps me refresh my mental habits. Less time with television helps me avoid the routine of either pondering the horror of the evening news or agonizing with the miseries of talk show guests.

Spiritual refreshment comes in all kinds of packages. The results refresh our soul when we find ways to listen to our Creator and live a life that pleases Him. Time spent refreshing our soul is time spent wisely and wonderfully.

Refresh your body, mind, and spirit regularly. Adapt the personal habit of refreshment!

Refocus and Focus and Refocus Some More

The process of evaluating and reevaluating who we are and how we plan to live our lives is a process that, when repeated regularly, will produce endless results. During this first year of retirement we have an all-encompassing opportunity to refocus our lives on the things that matter. We have the wisdom, the power, and the lifestyle transitional experience that retirement offers to cement the habit of refocusing.

I like to think of it as regularly looking at ourselves through rose-colored binoculars. Using the rose-colored lenses, we make sure to brighten our self-image in order to see ourselves in the best possible light. We adjust our setting to truly examine all our potential and to create a future that is all that we want it to be. We tackle self-improvement with enthusiasm and understand our ability to reap the rewards by repeating the process. We know we can, and undoubtedly will, keep getting better and better and better—so we repeat the process and refocus and focus and refocus some more.

Chapter 8

Self-Identity – Who Am I Now That I Have Retired?

Who am I now that I have retired? is a question that often needs some serious contemplation. The primary roles in our lives have defined us throughout the stages of our existence. As children we were daughters or sons, extensions of our parents. We knew ourselves only as connected to those whose love encompassed us. We grew in our own personality. We went to school and became students and became ballplayers or ballerinas. At first our self-identity was something we borrowed from make-believe and, yet, it still seemed to fit us, and we began the process of developing our individuality—our unique selves.

Some of us were shy and others quite outgoing; some of us were talkative and some rather quiet. And some were brave and welcomed new adventure while others were careful and tended to need Mom's reassurance.

Yes this thinking takes us a long way back, but perhaps going all the way back to our own beginning helps us to recognize and value the traits we've carried with us throughout our lives. Now many of those traits, the personality traits we had as little children, have stayed with us and have strongly influenced our life and our relationships as we moved from childhood to adulthood, from teenager to college student, from someone's child to someone's spouse to someone's parent. Now, a lifetime later, our personality continues to define who we are while exploring our own identity.

We move on and take our personality with us. Retirement will be what we want it to be, and it needs to fit to be fulfilling and rewarding. For most of us, our work life was probably quite compatible with our personality, or at least it didn't contradict it. The level of involvement with other people during our work day and the leader or follower relationship with coworkers (formally or informally) most likely worked pretty well for us.

If our work clearly defined our self-worth or self-image, we need to find ways to replicate this contributing factor of our self-fulfillment in our retirement. Without it we will feel a void—the same kind of void some couples experience when their children leave home. The restless-retirement syndrome can be compared to the empty-nest syndrome. Something is missing. Sure we don't have to get up and go to work every day, and that should be good news. However, it really depends a lot on what we do instead. It depends on how well our self-identity is established in a manner that suits us.

Our childhood formed our personality. The events of adulthood coincided with our identity. A good match meant a good life. Now, in retirement, we may need to find new ways to create the match. And, on the other hand, if adulthood up to now wasn't all that great, we'll do well to go back to our roots and recognize and value our true God-given identity.

29

I'm not suggesting that we adapt a "that's just the way I am" attitude. However, a self-awareness of our basic personality traits gives us insight to personal fulfillment. Our life activities need to compliment our true selves in a way that confirms our identity.

Insight to Personal Fulfillment

I am rather outgoing and have a need for self-expression. I am conscientious and purposeful and drawn to adventure but not brave or bold. I like myself best when optimistic and proactive, but it's necessary to give myself a push to get started and then again to keep going. I have the capacity to take charge and can be a bit bossy and opinionated. Sometimes I take on more than my share, overextending myself and letting other people's problems become my own. There's a need to create a balance and listen to the advice of my family when they see me going off the deep end and becoming all consumed with something I want to change or fix. It is important to me to make a contribution to the world—to make a difference. I need to know that I am helping others and being a positive influence. I want to know that at least a few other people are living a happier, more fulfilled life because of me.

This is me and how I see myself. I challenge you to do the same and write at least ten sentences describing yourself, your strongest personality traits, tendencies, and ambitions. You'll find instructions in the Appendix, page 97, to guide you in an exercise that will help define your identity.

Chapter 9

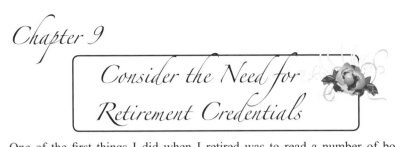

Consider the Need for Retirement Credentials

One of the first things I did when I retired was to read a number of books about retirement. I remember being surprised when more than one author suggested that I might need a title in retirement. I would need a new response to the commonly asked question, "So what do you do?"

As I quickly understood, yes it is true that nothing ages you more quickly than when you say "I am retired now but I used to work for XYZ Company as an ABC specialist." Rule number one is this: Never, ever talk about yourself in past tense. We have stopped working; we didn't stop living. Past-tense self-identity only applies after we're dead, and even then it represents how others describe us not how we see ourselves.

I really thought this whole concept was crazy the first time I read it but, believe me, it is true. We all need a response to the question, "So what do you do?" I strongly encourage you to figure it out and start using it today. The point is that it is perfectly OK to say that you are retired, but it's not OK to describe yourself only in terms of what you used to do.

My husband and I are retired and now we are enjoying traveling.

I'm retired and I spend a lot of time with my grandchildren.

I'm a golfer.

I'm retired and now I'm a volunteer for…

I'm a freelance…

Talk about your work with the church, with your favorite charity, or with a hobby. It really doesn't matter how we introduce ourselves, but the point is that we need to give ourselves a *current* identity.

This was a pretty big issue for me. In fact, one of the first things that I did was to create a resume that has been adjusted numerous times to reflect not only my achievements and credentials but also my current interests and ambitions. Since I was leaning towards some type of free-lance work and hadn't yet figured out what I wanted to do, I needed a resume. It gave me a starting place, an inventory of my self-worth. The format I use allows me to summarize my experience and focus on my interests. If you plan to work during your retirement, or even if you don't, use my template to create your own experience and interests' inventory. (Note: See worksheet in Appendix, page 99.)

Put Yourself on Paper

We've talked about establishing our priorities in Chapter Three. We've defined our self-identity in Chapter Eight. And now we consider the value of putting together an experience and interests' inventory. I've included all three of these exercises in the Appendix starting on page 93 to help you get in touch with yourself. The process of putting it on paper helps us to put the pieces together so that we can step back and see ourselves more clearly.

Retirement gives us the opportunity to reinvent ourselves. We walk into this new stage of life with maturity, experience, wisdom, and integrity. Life is what it is right now. If we've messed up in the past (and that's probably so), it's time to do what can be done to fix it—fix it or let it go. If there are fences to mend, let's mend them—forgive or be forgiven, let's try to get it done. To do retirement right, we need to figure out our action plan and commit ourselves to acting on that plan.

Before moving on to Stage Three, we need to celebrate the first-year anniversary of our retirement and plan to celebrate it each and every year. Why not? After all, birthdays, wedding anniversaries, and even the years we've had with any given company are celebrated. Let's celebrate retirement too and hope it will continue to be rewarding and last a long, long time.

On May 23, 2006, I retired and to celebrate my retirement success, it's time to stop and take stock of how this first year went. It's been a good year and I've had fun. In my own small way, I think I've even contributed to making this world a better place. I've been a little nicer person, a little kinder and, hopefully, more thoughtful. There is a satisfaction in whom I am becoming and a readiness to move forward. There's still a lot to learn, but I'm confident my second year of retirement will be better than my first.

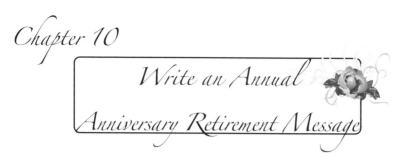

Chapter 10

Write an Annual Anniversary Retirement Message

To help secure my own retirement success, year after year, I've decided to keep a retirement journal. In my work life, the performance appraisal process was a very important and valuable process that helped me to help myself and help others celebrate their accomplishments of the past year and set realistic expectations for the year ahead.

For many years before I retired, I wrote an annual summary of my accomplishments and contributions to the success of my business. I introduced this process in my company as part of our performance appraisal process. It was helpful for me and it was helpful for many other employees and managers.

There is good value in this process, and I've decided to take the process into my future. I'll summarize my accomplishments and contributions each year during retirement. I'll keep messages in a journal so I can go back each year, see where I've been and, therefore, it will help me decide where I'm going.

The retirement journal will tell my story. It will be encouraging, not critical. The journal will help me move forward armed with self-awareness and good intentions. The process to write a retirement anniversary message is found on page 101 in the Appendix.

Retirement, a Status Symbol

Having explored the thoughts of retirement credentials and retirement identity, we have developed a better understanding of the importance of avoiding past-tense self-imaging. We've worked on creating a personal identity that fits our personality and the kind of retirement life that is attractive to us. Now we are beginning to see our retirement life as a life that will meet our own expectations.

Others may see their retirement as proof of financial security. Just as some people see their work life as a paycheck that pays the bills. If there's enough money to live on without being employed, then they can retire. If they've got enough money or enough resources for income without working, they're all set. It's that simple for some people.

However, I suspect that if you are reading this book, then it is not quite so cut and dry for you. Like me, you are looking for a retirement life with value and purpose. You are interested in exploring the options before retirement and perhaps also during the first years of retirement, just as I am doing. Your first anniversary retirement message will be written and saved for posterity. You'll get ready to move forward concentrating on making every day count.

Stage Three

Moving Forward

Now as experienced retirees we are ready to move forward, recognizing that all five stages of retirement have both positive and negative sides. Although this book focuses on my life experiences and the positive aspects of adult development, it is important to recognize (in both ourselves and in others) the fact that we have options. We can choose to set ourselves up for a positive retirement, or we can choose to stay stagnant, stuck in a world of status quo. Moving forward, these will be our choices and the cornerstones of our future.

Value and purpose can be chosen versus a future of "I-wish-I-had . . ." regrets. We can determine to have wisdom and maturity and diligently turn away from our own tendencies towards immature, self-centeredness. As we act with passion and energy, we can reject idleness and boredom. It is our choice to continue to learn and teach and enjoy the rewards of becoming mentors.

In doing so, we'll promise to give our family and friends the best of ourselves—a truly wonderful legacy.

Please join me in choosing:

Value and Purpose

Wisdom and Maturity

Passion and Energy

Learning and Teaching

Chapter 11

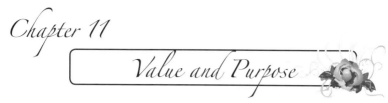

Value and Purpose

The Best Keep Getting Better and Better and Better

In the business world I was an executive—a senior vice president of my company, and I knew that the success of our business was in the hands of the people under my leadership. I tried to focus my attention and energy on developing other people. One year at our annual staff seminar, I introduced the concept, "And the best keep getting better and better and better." Introducing the Outstanding Achievement Awards, I incorporated this message into my presentation, "And the best keep getting better and better and better." Our staff responded with enthusiasm, and as I repeated the lead-in to the phrase, "And the best keep getting better," the entire group joined in completing my sentence "better and better." Before my presentation was over, the group was leading the chant.

This message became a company slogan, and year after year veteran employees and new employees joined in. It was fun and it was meaningful. Our slogan helped people feel appreciated and put value on our team. It was repeated often in business meetings, in managers meetings, and in customer service training programs.

Now I bring this message into our retirement development strategy. We need to embrace the concept and reinforce ourselves and each other. The best really can keep getting better and better and better. And, committing ourselves to self-improvement, we add value and purpose to who we are and will become in retirement.

We have the opportunities that retirement living presents to us. Choosing to set aside some of the busyness of life, we can focus on the things that really matter most. We support our own cause by stopping, if only ever so briefly, to contemplate our true values that give meaning to our lives.

My husband is the most important person in the world to me. We've lived together in some fashion of marital bliss for nearly forty years. Only God knows how long we will continue together on this earth. We are a team, a team that at its personality core has two individuals who are very different. I am outgoing and spontaneous. He is quiet and reserved, yet confident and strongly focused on values that we share—our kids, our grandkids, and our mothers take center stage in our lives.

We were raised to be people of integrity and honesty, and we raised our children to those same standards. Ray is a doer and a fixer. He helps out on the family farm that his brother owns and helps the neighbors when their lawn mower needs fixing. He can fix pretty much anything and his kids have a To Do List of handyman stuff waiting for him when we visit. Even the grandkids already know where to take a broken toy for quick repairs.

I am a helper too. I love spending time helping friends and family members with resume writing or solving a business problem. I like to try to help people build self-esteem, and I am good at giving support and encouragement to those who need it.

We both keep close contact with our mothers and spend a good deal of time caring for their needs and enjoying their company.

We Are Parents to Our Children, Not Their Best Friends

Blessed with three wonderful daughters and sons-in-law, we value our relationship with them and all ten of our grandchildren. We are glad to sometimes give them a helping hand and proud that they really don't need one. We are parents to our children, not their best friends. Although always there when they need us, we try not to meddle in their lives too much.

We respect them as adults and expect them to live up to our expectations. Thank God, they do. Our home is a playland for our grandchildren with swing set and slide and a hot tub that quickly becomes a kiddy pool when they visit. Our life has value and purpose. We know that, as the years go on, life will change, but at our core will be a need to find ways to help others and give encouragement and support to those who need it.

Chapter 12

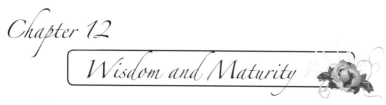

Wisdom and Maturity

From infant to toddler, from childhood to adolescence, from teenager to twenty-something, our life began and the seeds of desire for maturity started to grow. Often with impatient expectations, we learned to look ahead and to anticipate each of our new beginnings.

Throughout our entire lives, and with each step of maturity, new opportunities await our eager exploration and inborn sense of adventure. It is all just a part of life. We are born, grow up, develop, learn, experience, and mature. We move forward and understand that each stage of maturity has new meaning and purpose for the rest of our lives.

Looking back on our past, we realize, that for some of us, the twenty-something became thirty-something before we even saw it coming. The birth of our children gave way to the joy of parenting and the awesome sense of responsibility that came with the territory.

Now much sooner than we imagined possible, our children are adults, and we begin to realize the gap between what they understand about maturity and what we are now living. We experience grandparenthood and retirement. We move forward, explore, and understand. Life presents a new set of choices and those choices become the cornerstone of our future.

Opportunities of Retirement Life

Retirement living presents opportunities to us. We can choose to set aside some of the busyness of life and focus on the things that really matter most. We support our own cause by stopping, if only ever so briefly, to contemplate the true values that give meaning to our lives.

God has a purpose for each of us in our lives. Personal experiences give us the maturity and the wisdom to understand His messages. Retirement gives us the opportunity to change focus or readjust our thinking as needed.

If we've lived on the fast track with too much attention on material things and getting ahead, we may have missed out on some of the riches of our lives. Perhaps, out of greed or necessity, our life was lived with a strong focus on climbing the corporate ladder and buying a new home or car.

For some of us there are some regrets. Now with wisdom and maturity we look back and wish some things had been done differently. We missed out. We messed up. But now, wiser and much more in tune to the world around us, it seems God speaks to us in a louder voice, or maybe we just started listening a little better.

The opportunities of retirement are endless. We have the wisdom and maturity to choose our destiny. Since I was a little girl (really as long as I can remember), I've carried within my heart a simple little prayer that I repeat often: *Dear God, help me to be all that you want me to be.* Now in retirement I begin to understand—I need to *keep my head on straight.* I need to *listen more.* I want to *try every day to become a better person.* I will be *better today than I was yesterday.* I'll do my best *to make today count.*

Life brings wisdom and maturity too. Take time to take stock of yourself. Where are you now and where do you want to be? Contemplate and complete the following thoughts for yourself.

I need to . . .

I want to . . .

I'll try to . . .

I will . . .

With wisdom and maturity, we move forward creating our "today" and building our "tomorrow."

Chapter 13

Passion and Energy

Passion energizes our existence. Passion is the push that propels us to dive into our future and the enthusiasm that encourages and empowers us to enjoy our present. Retirement is all about creating today and finding tomorrow. It's about living life to its fullest. With passion and energy, we consciously exit the chaotic world of yesterday with all its exuberance and busyness and choose to follow a dream with determination to turn that dream into a chosen reality.

As I write I feel energized because I am in the process of self-discovery. I walked into retirement life with my eyes wide open and with a strong desire to make my retirement the best it can possibly be. My desire is to make a difference in my own life and in the lives of others. I've stumbled into my mission and found passion and energy.

I'm writing a book and am truly surprised at myself. Oh, I've always enjoyed writing and teaching and motivational speaking that's been geared at helping other people. But now in retirement I've settled into a new niche—writing with passion and energy. Personal inspiration comes from within is my belief. When we open our minds and hearts and souls to discovery and we share those discoveries with others in the process, we discover ourselves and encourage others to discover themselves too.

I have a passion for life and a sense of adventure. I delight in the opportunity to step into the world of our grandchildren and to try to explore the world from their viewpoint.

Marveling at wisdom and insight, I am inspired by life's revelations that are so profoundly spoken by my young adult children. Their energy for life is contagious, and I'm proud of who they are and who they are becoming. I welcome the occasional opportunity they give me to speak with maturity and with the wisdom of a parent who's *been there*.

Having strong convictions about the importance of letting my daughters make their own decisions, I feel passionate enough to encourage our friends and siblings to step back and allow their grown children space. Parents of adult children need to trust them to do their best and to realize that *their bes*t is most often better than *our best* once was. Their best is good enough, and they can move forward responsibly without unsolicited parental guidance.

My relationship with those I love makes me feel passionate and energized. Many years ago when I was a teenager and falling into the typical high school habit of best friends and social clicks, I remember my father responding to a conversation my best friend and I were having that was clearly critical of another classmate. When my friend was out of ear shot and it was just Dad and me, my dad reminded me, "Karen, you know I've always been proud of you because you've always had a special way of looking for the good in other people."

I was definitely embarrassed because Dad's words caught me right in the midst of our discussion. Looking back now, I don't even remember what the criticism was or even who we were gossiping about, but I clearly remember feeling ashamed of myself. Dad's words reminded me that I was better than that. Mom and Dad taught us to like ourselves and when we found good in ourselves, we also found good in other people. We were raised to be optimistic and to be passionate and enthusiastic about life. I still really want to be an optimist and try to be one.

Trying to Be a True Optimist

A true optimistic thinker is someone who regularly counts his blessings and therefore realizes he is truly blessed. He sees the good around him even when it's hard to find and the world seems engulfed in hurt, anger, sorrow, or sadness. The optimist looks beyond. The optimist anticipates good things and sorts out the bad to keep it all in perspective. When something bad happens, an optimist feels the pain, but then he moves on trying not to dwell on negative things too long.

When we find our passion and our energy, we find a hidden treasure—the light of hope, joy, and happiness; the dawn of new beginnings; the passion and energy of life. It's there for all of us to find. Let's find it in our lives, hobbies, interests, mission, adventures, and relationships.

Pondering the topic of the passion and energy of life, I enjoy the adventure of trying to search within my soul. I read and reread the eloquent and insightful words of Harry Emerson Fosdick in his essay, The Privilege of Living.

Speaking to my readers of passion and energy, I realize I find my own in reading. I travel from writer to reader and reader to writer to try to capture the meaning of goodness and rightful living that touches my heart and soul.

It was a wonderful life I spoke of just pages ago: the chaotic, busy life of the career woman that was once mine. I knew passion and energy in that life, but now my passion joins hands with the new life I'm now living. I love the adventure of traveling in a world of discovery. I understand the goodness, kindness, and rightful living that Fosdick speaks of as a privilege, not an obligation. I feel passion and energy that comes from simple things in life.

Understanding the Privilege of Life

Yesterday Ray and I spent the day with our moms. It was a day that repeats itself often at this stage of their lives and ours. Both our moms are doing quite well in conquering and adjusting to some quite annoying physical limitations.

My mom is limited by her emphysema which now requires the support of oxygen around the clock. With determination for independence, Mom strives to learn to handle her portable Helios machine and to stick to her regiment of breathing treatments and medicines. My mother-in-law is quite crippled with arthritis and her vision has failed to the point of seeing only blurred images. Both our moms are to be admired and both help me to better understand the privilege of life.

Our day began with an outing to take Ray's mom to see her sister, Aunt Ruthie, in the nursing home and then later that evening we picked up my mom to join us for dinner at a local restaurant. As our day came to an end, Mom asked about Aunt Ruthie and was pleased that our visit with her was good, and Mom was happy for Mabel (Ray's Mom) knowing how relieved she was to find Aunt Ruthie doing well.

Aunt Ruthie has only lived in the nursing home for a few months now, but with the support of her family who try to visit often and the help of her physical therapist and nurses, she is improving beyond medical expectations.

She professes contentment, telling us that it's good to no longer have to worry about things like grocery shopping, cooking, medication, or paying bills. She sleeps a lot and boasts of being mostly free of pain. Encouraged by the results of her therapy, she sees progress in her physical capabilities and even in her own outlook. The birds outside her window and the flowers her kids brought give her enjoyment. Asking for her eye glasses perched on top of her Bible on the dresser, she enjoyed the photos of the family reunion.

Although she really didn't want to give up her apartment (and I am sure still weighs the possibility of returning to live there), Aunt Ruthie sees the goodness in her current situation. Her mind is clear and she sees around her reasons to rejoice in such a blessing. She feels safe, cared for, and loved.

Probably considered poor by financial measurements and by most people's view of quality of life, she knows that her days here on earth are most likely very limited—but she is rich in soul. Although I doubt that Aunt Ruthie is really afraid of dying, she seems content to enjoy the privilege of living today. I see a feeble body that strives to help us understand that she's OK now. I see Ray's mom who's very happy to see her sister doing so much better than at her last visit months ago. I am encouraged for my own mom, and I better understand the goodness of life that gives me passion and energy. I found it in a place I would have never expected.

Chapter 14
Learning and Teaching

It's time to be a student again. To live a life that is rich with meaning is to live a life that continuously seeks new knowledge, new skills, and a better understanding of topics with which we already have some experience. Our choice of subjects is endless and our need to learn is essential and everlasting.

If you are retired and working part time, undoubtedly you'll have the opportunity to learn on the job. New knowledge will broaden your horizons. Continuing education classes at a local college will offer some interesting subjects and the opportunity to meet some new interesting people too.

Also, in retirement we will do well to strive to keep our technical skills up to date. I needed a computer class and was glad I found *Microsoft Office for Dummies*. I learned a lot and knew improved computer skills were necessary to support my other interests. Even keeping up with the technology of cell phones can be a challenge for some of us baby boomers, and I'm glad the folks at the mall are pretty patient and available for one-on-one coaching sessions.

Craft stores, home decorating centers, libraries, and community centers all offer some interesting classes too. And to my way of thinking, aerobics, yoga, and pilates all qualify as higher education especially for retirees who have a tendency toward being couch potatoes.

I'm not a golfer but I know many people over fifty who enjoy endless hours trying to learn to keep their head down and perfect their swing. Even the knowledge of the language of golf—knowing a birdie from a bogie and what's so great about being under par—makes us a better listener when we are in the company of our golfing buddies.

At this point, I guess I am a casual student, and I enjoy taking a class or two in the spring and in the fall. I take continuing education classes and I like taking classes on campus. However, the possibilities of being an on-line student are endless, and even those who live in remote areas can pursue their studies on line. I admire other retirees who are out there earning degrees—just for the sake of learning and the satisfaction of the accomplishment. Education (formal or informal) is an important component of an enriched existence.

I believe that every subject that we pursue as a student, we'll have the opportunity to use. Grade school kids learning history and high school kids studying algebra may feel they disagree with me on this, but somehow maturity gives me a real sense of value for everything I learn. I know I only retain a small portion of everything I take in, but that small portion is mine to keep and to share with others when it is beneficial and the opportunity presents itself.

In retirement we want others to look to us as a source of knowledge and a teacher of know-how. We have an obligation to educate and a calling to pass on our wisdom to those who seek it.

A Message to Couples About Learning

I lived a very busy career life and, at the same time, I always tried to make room for my three daughters. When they were little, I had the good fortune to be a stay-at-home mom and it was great. However, as they grew up, I became a career woman and it seems each year from the time they were ten, twelve, and fourteen on, my career expanded and juggling family and career became more and more a challenge.

I know I missed out on some important stuff with my girls, and I have some regrets about that, but on the flip side, I also always knew they were always well-grounded in core values. They knew they were loved unconditionally and forever. They were and will always be strong and independent, capable and self-reliant.

The three of them are very close to each other and experience sisterhood at its best. I hope not just out of necessity, but they seemed to learn to count on each other to see them through. Especially during their college days, Ray and I were glad they were all going to the same school and even shared the same apartment much of the time. We used to say it gave us comfort to know they watched out for each other, and we were encouraged to think that at least one of them usually had her head on straight at any given time.

Ray, in some ways, always seemed to handle his own career juggling act much better than I did. He often picked up the slack and took on household finances and extended parenting responsibilities quite naturally.

When the girls were in high school and in college, I traveled quite a lot on business. Ray held down the fort at home and managed to keep a pretty close eye on the girls even when they were away at college. In addition, he was a constant source of know-how for them and taught them skills that gave them female independence.

They lived together and then on their own, and each of them developed careers before they married and began raising families of their own. Their husbands marvel at the practical know-how each of them possesses—the skills they learned and cultivated from the guidance of their father.

They can hang a picture or build a shelf or even do minor lawn mower repairs and mow the lawn themselves if need be. They even learned to change a tire and to use jumper cables to recharge the car battery when necessary. As all three of them would agree, Dad rescued them when needed and yet still taught them to be quite resourceful.

On the other hand, Ray mostly pampers me. I wouldn't know where to begin to change a tire, and I hardly ever hang a picture without his assistance. However, we've decided to make some changes and now Ray is beginning to take me on as a student too. I sometimes even pay the bills and go to the bank. I know the passwords and can transfer money from one account to another online.

We battle a bit sometimes on the whole learning process with Ray, the teacher, and with me, the student, but we're doing it. And, actually, we are surprising ourselves, and we are finding that most of the time its fun to try to switch roles and test our skills. In the end I think we will probably even learn to appreciate each other more. For sure, I am amazed at all the stuff Ray does that I honestly have never really paid much attention to.

Ray and I both hope we'll live a long and happy retirement life together, but we also know that unless I increase my independence and practical knowledge on the many subjects that he has just taken care of, I'll struggle a lot with day-to-day living without him.

I'm learning things that, hopefully, I'll never need to know, but I do know that now is the time to learn them. Married couples need to teach each other skills of single survival that either he or she will use someday. We'll struggle enough when our partner is gone; let's not struggle with finding keys or passwords or bank accounts.

Learning and teaching go hand-in-hand. We have a lifelong responsibility to pursue both endeavors. The opportunity to learn encompasses every other opportunity we have in life. Curiosity and interest prompts our intellect to seek and to find new information and to claim it for our own. Everything we do, read, and think about becomes a source of education. "You've got to use it or you'll lose it" is a philosophy that applies to everything we learn. "You've got to teach it to master it" applies to all the subjects we are most interested in.

On the subject of teaching, I've come to the conclusion that teaching in all of its forms is a privilege and responsibility given to all mankind. Others will learn from us. It's inevitable. What we learn and how we pass on information will be our legacy.

In my career life, I had the responsibility to develop company managers and trainers. I knew that my success depended on the results produced by the leaders I trained and all the people who worked for us and with us to make our business successful. To that end, many years ago I created a training model that incorporated the key concepts of teaching as I know them. They are MODEL, TEACH, PRACTICE, ASSESS, and COACH. I've used these concepts as the foundation of all the teaching and training programs that I have implemented.

Every new-employee training, every managers training, sales training, or customer service workshop—every type of skill development program that we offered included a mixture of these methods. I've carried the methods into my own life and consciously used them to teach my children and my grandchildren too. What you are teaching or who your students are doesn't really matter. The awareness and use of these methods will help your students learn.

The objective is to adapt the methods to fit the student's learning style and the content of whatever you want to teach and your student wants to learn. Teaching is a part of who I am and I believe it needs to be a part of every retiree's purpose in life. As mature adults, we are destined to teach, and our teaching influences the future of the world around us.

Chapter 15

Model, Teach, Practice, Assess, and Coach

To elaborate a little further, I will walk through each method:

Modeling is the process of demonstrating—of showing others how to do something. It encompasses all the process that people who learn by watching use. We teach by modeling when we take two shoestrings and tie a bow while our five-year-old grandson closely observes. We model everything we teach intentionally or even unintentionally. Our behavior, attitudes, and skills are modeled regularly for others to see and replicate if they are so inclined to do so.

Retirement living offers us lots of teaching opportunities. As parents, grandparents, and mature adults, many other people pay attention to what we say and do. Hopefully, we're on the right path in life, and we know some stuff that others want to learn. Modeling can teach by accident and can be very effective, or modeling can serve as a real teaching method of its own. We model when we take the time to demonstrate the things we know step-by-step and in a deliberate way, repeating the process as many times as needed until our student can follow our lead and make a skill his own.

We take teaching to another level and open the possibility of learning to many more students when we add directional teaching to our criteria. We teach by telling and by giving step-by-step instructions, breaking our lessons down and describing each step with clear, descriptive words. Another method, the teaching method, is born and when it suits the learning style of our pupils, the lightbulbs of discovery begin to shine.

Next we add practice to our teaching format. Some people learn best by doing, and for them the practice sessions are very necessary for skill development. Remember when you teach others to create an environment where practice, even imperfect practice, is encouraged. A sloppy, floppy bow on our five-year-old grandson's sneaker is just a practice run, but with encouragement from a grandpa, his teacher, it will improve before your very eyes. When teaching someone something (and it doesn't matter what it is), try to allow the learner freedom to practice, freedom to fail at first, and freedom to try again.

Sometimes learners get stuck and it is the job of the teacher to help them get unstuck. That's where the assessing method plays its part. As a teacher, we support the learning process but also watch and assess the progress of the practicing learner. Our assessment becomes our coaching points, the guidance that great teachers give to help their students do their best.

As we move on in our retirement life, let's realize our true potential to teach others things we know. Let's develop the methods that produce the best results. If we consciously incorporate all five components—model, teach, practice, assess, and coach—we will be great teachers and the best will keep getting better and better and better. Retirement gives us the mission and the vision to learn and to teach. Even if you have never thought of yourself as a student or as a teacher before, I encourage you to take the challenge. The value of your learning promises ever-growing self-worth. The rewards of your teaching will someday be someone's priceless inheritance. What will you learn and how will you grow? What do you know and who will you teach?

Stage Four

Live Life!

As we move into the happily-ever-after stage of retirement, we move forward with a plan to support our personal vision of a life that is going to be all that we want it to be—not because it'll be perfect or predictable, but because we're ready. We've learned a lot about ourselves and how we want to live our lives.

We know we will need to apply what we've learned and redirect our process as necessary. The quality of our life is ours to claim. Unknown territory lies ahead. We think that we are in pretty good shape to venture out secure in the knowledge of who we are and what kind of things we value as important to our future.

Chapter 16
Live Your Life in Balance

A simple, quiet day at home; a busy, demanding day devoted to volunteer work; or a purposeful day focused on solving a family crisis—each of these days will be a part of our life that repeats itself often during the life of retirement. Earlier we talked about the benefit of creating a balance in our lives. As we move on concentrating on living our life to the fullest, we do well to check and recheck our state of balance periodically.

We do well to realize and to understand that living our life to the fullest happens when we balance out all of life's activities. We add satisfaction to our lives when we are living in balance.

We need to avoid any tendency to overload our day-to-day living with the clutter of meaningless activity. In his book, *The Tests of Character,* Harry Emerson Fosdick talks about the importance of putting first things first in life. He talks about, "the commonest failures in character—the crowding out of things that really matter by things that do not matter much." He encourages his readers to recognize a tendency to go about their lives focused on meaningless chatter. He compares the busyness of life that many people lead to a child's doll stuffed with sawdust.

If every day we just go-go-go and push-push-push ourselves to the point of exhaustion, we'll grow weary and tired long before our time. I don't know if this is a "guy thing" or what, but I find it interesting that my husband bucks when life gets too hectic just as I remember my father doing.

As a typical routine, Ray and I start our day early every morning, often allowing early morning hours to ponder the sunrise as we enjoy our morning coffee. He enjoys the sunrise anticipating his activities of the day. I combine reading time and often time to start my writing. Usually, a calendar of activities requires an early morning alarm clock that nudges us up and out the door by 7:00 two or three days a week, and that works really well for us. However, when our schedule gets crazy and those two or three early morning outings hit two or three days in a row, Ray will react and revolt pulling the reins in on what he clearly sees as hectic craziness.

A life in balance for us allows us the pleasure of a lazy morning as part of our usual routine at least a couple of days each week. Other days we like to get going early and especially enjoy frequent day trips to spend time with our grandchildren. In addition, I like to plan some kind of excursion at least once a month.

In the past we always vacationed, but most of the time family-life and work-life responsibilities took priority, and vacation time was limited to one or two weeks each year with a few long weekends that we tagged on over a long holiday or after a business trip. Now vacation time comes more frequently. In fact, I find I like a trip on my calendar to look forward to about every six to eight weeks. It doesn't have to be anything too special but just a few days to get away and enjoy a change of scenery and a little adventure. In a few weeks we'll pack up our bikes and head up north wandering our way along the shores of Lake Michigan and peddling our way from one little town to another along the bicycle trails we discovered there years ago.

Special occasions and family gatherings are always on our schedule. This month it's a birthday party for our grandson Miles' first birthday, a family gathering to participate in the Food Allergy Anaphylaxis Network Walk, and a surprise party to unveil the *Recipes and Stories* book that we created for Ray's Mom.

For me, living life to the fullest requires some excitement and some fun things to do. It's important to find ways to explore during retirement and to take advantage of the freedom of the extra time retirement living offers us.

Chapter 17

Life Is a Gift

As we each go about our retirement life, we need to take special care in how we spend our time. It's just way too easy to let time drift away year after year and find ourselves looking back wondering what we did and regretting what we didn't do. Life is a gift that needs to be cherished. What we do with our life, how we spend our time, and how we use our talents are decisions of our choosing. We decide what's important to us. We decide what really matters.

For some of us, as we turn the pages, the story of our life seems already written. Sometimes the circumstances of life seem to dictate our destiny. Some things are for sure out of our control and maybe even out of our reach. However, the power to make choices and the decision to make our choices wisely belongs to each of us.

Living our life to the fullest is easiest when we are healthy and able. In early years of retirement, many of us may take our state of life quite for granted. Good health and the physical ability to do pretty much anything we want to do have always been part of our life. Routine doctor checkups come and go uneventful, if we are lucky. Our diet and exercise habits are motivated by vanity and the scale, more than by any real commitment to good health.

However, at some point most of us will clearly see the connection between our diet and exercise habits and our ability to live our life to its fullest. We learn to eat healthier. We concentrate on keeping our cholesterol and blood pressure down. We eliminate caffeine and we start drinking more water. And, interestingly enough, most of us begin to realize that how we eat affects how we feel, and how we feel effects our decision to live our life to the fullest.

If we're smart, we increase our physical activity and we see measurable results. Life is good! We appreciate its fullness and realize living is a privilege and how we live is a choice.

Now, I speak for all my friends and family members with chronic illness, and I acknowledge the reality of the situation. Either now or in the future, chronic illness, disease, or physical limitations may be a part of life for each of us. It may limit us and interfere with our choices. Medical science can guide us in ways to improve or help us maintain a better quality of life. When necessary, we may need to call on our own determination to help us adjust to the limitations that can be beyond our control. However, let's make sure we know what is really beyond our control and out of the reach of medical help.

Yes, it is true that some of us will discover that there are some things that we will just have to live with, but we shouldn't just accept those things too quickly. Too many people over sixty and even more people over seventy or eighty tend to give in to chronic illness, disease, or physical limitations too easily. Let's decide to persistently seek medical help and explore all our options. We can determine to find ways to improve our situation. Let's change the situation or find ways to work around our challenges and to look beyond our obstacles. Living our life to the fullest is a challenge, and thousands of people are finding wonderful ways to move beyond their personal barriers.

Chapter 18

Contributions and the Feeling of Being Needed

Living your life to the fullest requires contributions and the feeling of being needed. It seems a bit ironic, but living your life to the fullest is not really about our life, but it's about the influence we have on the quality of someone else's life. Contributions and the feeling of being needed—spend time considering where you stand on the subject and you'll realize the connection. Living your life to the fullest requires a personal awareness of contributions you are currently making to the quality of someone else's life that gives you a feeling of being needed.

Encouragement gives others strength. Who needs our encouragement and how freely do we give it?

A lively discussion on topics of mutual interest rejuvenates a tired soul. Who do we talk with and what do we talk about?

An hour or two devoted to the *Cat in the Hat* and a Candy Land match with grandchildren can be the contribution that reaps rewards in multiple directions. The little ones enjoy the attention. The parents appreciate the grandchild and grandparent relationship. The grandparent's life is energized.

We look for, find, and value the opportunity to make contributions to the quality of life of someone else and we feel needed. The opportunity presents itself regularly when we learn to look for it.

Contributions Come Quietly From Within

Sometimes, we know that our contributions and the feeling of being needed come quietly from within. It's the calming, comforting peace we feel in our hearts when we pray and talk to God about our worries and woes. Somehow we know that He listens, and He will make things better for someone we love. Our prayers are our contributions, and they give us the feeling of being needed. Everyone needs someone to pray for them.

We know people who are tired of praying or too weary and discouraged to pray, especially for themselves. Our prayers can be the contribution that helps them to pray and to know that God is near.

I write with a renewed commitment to prayer, and a realization that my prayers will ask God to give strength to the souls of those prayed for. I pray for peace for the elderly, who are fearful of dying, frightened by anxiety, and tormented by loneliness. I'll pray for them and find ways to brighten their day. This will be my contribution, and I'll reap the rewards of a feeling of being needed. My prayers are needed. And I can help others to pray too.

Our contributions may seem rather small; they may only impact the lives of a few. Or they can be worldly and powerful and remarkable—we may even earn prestige and recognition from our contributions. However, all we contribute, grand or small, will fill our lives with richness and fulfillment.

No one needs to know what we do. It really doesn't matter. Over time, and with practice, contributions and the feeling of being needed will become who we are and how we live our lives. It's a great feeling to contribute and to know that others need us. We create that feeling simply by giving of ourselves—consciously, willingly, and unconditionally. Oh, what a wonderful way to live our lives to the fullest!

Chapter 19

Lightheartedness and Laughter

On one hand, I've talked a lot about the importance of living a meaningful life. However, on the other hand, I must also emphasize and encourage all of us to insert a refreshing amount of lightheartedness into our day-to-day living. Let's not take ourselves too seriously in this business of living our life to the fullest.

A true joy of retirement is the opportunity to allow ourselves to linger in the land of lightheartedness on a regular basis. As adults, we have probably lived long enough to consider our past experiences as a lifetime of experiences. We have already lived a full life—seen a lot and done a lot. Yet now in retirement, we can (and probably should) experiment with some new and improved approaches to our own humble existence.

We've talked about adventure and explored our identity for a deeper understanding of who we are, wondering and pondering the reality of life and the spirituality of our own being. We learn and teach and avoid any personal tendency to preach. Wisdom is found in our own maturity.

And now we learn how to linger in our own lightheartedness. It makes me smile to myself when I realize that lingering in lightheartedness doesn't always come so naturally. I look around and find examples of some retirees who seldom linger and others who linger lightheartedly quite effortlessly. If it is already a habit, let's capture it and if not, let's acquire it. For those of us who are still students of lighthearted lingering, we need to explore our options.

Learning how to linger in lightheartedness takes a bit of concentration at first. After all, some of us have quite often passed by our opportunities to smile hundreds of times in a day without even noticing the little things that prompt a grin. Probably little children, especially our own grandchildren, present us with our best material. All we have to do is take a moment to watch them, listen, and catch the contagious smile in their eyes. Little ones are naturally fun loving. We just need to take a moment to observe their playful ways.

For my husband Ray, birds, squirrels, and the neighbor's cat playing in the yard present wonderful lighthearted lingering opportunities. Smile swapping and friendly casual greetings with strangers on the street just take a second and brighten everyone's day. Time spent with others with a sense of humor and even clumsy attempts at repeating funny stories produce smiling results for the storyteller as well as the listener.

E-mail joke sharing with long-distance friends can help us cultivate the habit of lighthearted lingering. However, beware of some of the stuff that comes in via e-mail that is just plain crude. If you know someone who sends you the kind of stuff that makes you shake your head instead of grin, just click, delete, and move on. Nobody needs jokes that belittle others. Humor at someone else's expense isn't fun. If we seek humor that is uplifting, not downgrading, we will enjoy the opportunity to linger in the land of lightheartedness, and we will create good feelings and add richness to our lives and to the lives of others too.

Pets, nature, little children, and babies are great material for lighthearted lingering, but remember grown-ups are fun too. Everyone loves to be with people with a good sense of humor, and just about any time a group of people gather just for fun, humor will perk up its fun-loving head for all of us to see and enjoy. Let's enjoy lingering in the land of lightheartedness often and invite others to join in our fun.

Avoid Retirement Living That Is Too Peaceful and Uninterrupted

If the sign says: "No Pets!" "No Children!" or "Please Be Quiet!" please beware. You could be entering a retirement community that's full of stick-in-the-mud fuddy-duddies. If you really want to live your life to the fullest, let the neighborhood kids cut through your yard and don't fuss about an occasional late-night party down the street. People need people who like to laugh, and living our life to the fullest includes lightheartedness and laughter.

Chapter 20

Live Your Life With Fullness

Living your life to the fullest is about being alive. We intentionally live a life that is good and rich and wonderful. Our life is all that we want it to be and all that it was meant to be.

Here are some thoughts to nudge us towards fullness of life:

Live with integrity.

Live with honor.

Live with family pride.

Live with purpose.

Live with love.

Live with character.

Live with compassion.

Live with distinction.

Live with destiny.

Live with vision.

Live with support.

Live being all that you can be.

Live and give generously.

Live with initiative.

Live with wonder.

Live and try to understand.

Live sharing yourself.

Live with appreciation.

Live with honesty.

Live giving support.

Live and be encouraging.

Live with curiosity.

Live with determination.

Live with amazement.

Live with a future.

Live for today.

Live anticipating tomorrow.

Live being nice.

Live with a caring heart.

Live looking for goodness.

Live courageously.

Live prayerfully.

Live and teach.

Live with passion.

Live with energy.

Live up to your own potential.

Live with style.

Live with tradition.

Live with true friendship.

Live and contribute.

Live and learn.

Live with fun.

Live with memories.

Live independently.

Live with trust.

Live with high expectations.

Live helping others.

Live with patience.

Live free of pain.

Live free of guilt.

Live with security.

Live with books.

Live with a feeling of being needed.

Live with laughter.

Live with children.

Live with the elderly.

Live with people your own age.

Live with a teenager.

Live being considerate of others.

Live with someone holy.

Live with spirit.

Live loving to be alive.

Live with hope.

Live with dreams.

Live with surprises.

Live with people you love.

Live with a smile.

Live free of prejudice.

Live with forgiveness.

Live with value.

Live a long life.

Live with happiness.

Live with inspiration.

Live believing in yourself.

Live to make a difference.

Live with self-improvement.

Live making good choices.

Live as an optimist.

Live with a mission.

Live becoming a better person.

Live inspiring others to be all they can be.

Live with dignity.

Live with unconditional love.

Live for yourself.

Live for others.

Live with God.

Live with success.

Live with faith.

Live and leave a legacy.

Live with generosity.

Live being kind.

Live with joy.

Live with enthusiasm.

We Will Become the Person We Want To Be

I am who I am and pretty pleased with how I've turned out so far. Financially secure with a lifestyle that meets my needs, rich with life's experiences, and grounded in the present—that's where I find myself, and that's where I want to be. Now I am deep in the process of living a life of contribution and meaning. With maturity I found wisdom and insight. I look around me and I find opportunity. When I look within my soul, I find goodness and contentment.

As I look ahead to this stage of retirement, I must tell this story. I write it with anticipation of how I really want my life to be. Since I am just in the beginning stages of my own retirement, it's necessary to share my dreams and my intentions, not my own first-hand experiences. For the real first-hand experiences that are so important to the value of this book, I turn to those who share their retirement experiences with me.

Stage Five

Leaving a Legacy

We begin to plot our course for eternity realizing that life on earth as we know it will someday come to an end. Then we will move on to an unknown but promised-to-be-wonderful place. What about those we leave behind? What do we want to leave them? Our thoughts and plans and prayers take us beyond all our yesterdays and into all of our tomorrows.

Let's contemplate together and reach out to our eternal future and to the world we will someday leave behind. We've lived with integrity and honesty. We'll leave a legacy that embraces the principles of life. We anticipate God's kingdom. We find and give hope, faith, and encouragement. We celebrate the *success of our retirement—the success of our lives.*

Chapter 21

Principles of Life

As we age and we gather our life experiences, a new level of maturity begins to truly reflect who we are now and who we will continue to become. We will continue to strive to be flexible and stay in tune with modern-day living. We'll realize that the world around us is mostly represented by a younger generation. Even our own perception of age will change drastically. Eighty and ninety will be much younger than eighty and ninety use to be. Things like physical ailments will become annoying reminders of the aging process. Yet, we'll look around to others we know and be encouraged by our own abilities, counting our blessings.

We will value our own mortality and the body parts that are still working pretty well. We'll compare our eyesight, hearing, ability to walk, and minds to others we know that may be less fortunate. We'll value life and be thankful for the quality of life we are living.

Our standard of living will be simple and we will develop a better appreciation of the pleasures of each morning. The principles that we live by will be steadfast and unshakable. We'll be committed to our children, our grandchildren, our great-grandchildren, and to other family and friends. We will love them all unconditionally. We'll pray harder and more often. We'll live with integrity and honesty and we'll have a clear view of the decay of family values that challenge and haunt the younger generation in ways that we never experienced.

Our focus will turn full face to our family and all our loved ones. We will know that our work on earth is waiting and that it will not be over—never as long as we live. We'll hold in our hearts insight and wisdom and a vision of what's really important in life. From our vantage point, we'll see it all so clearly and always be eager to gently prod those around us in the right direction.

For sure, some of the world believes that at eighty or ninety, we will begin to experience a different relationship with our children. And, although there may be some reality in the circumstances, I challenge the thinking that suggests that someday we'll need help from our children *more,* and they'll need help from us *less.* Certainly, on the surface, I'm sure there is some truth about our aging and the unwelcomed limitations the process presents. Undoubtedly, we will need to be more careful and not clutter our minds or tax our bodies with tasks like housework, yard work, bill paying, and such. We will struggle a bit with the loss of freedom that delegating those duties might suggest.

However, it'll be time for us to give away some of this stuff and trade it in for a more important mission that we now need to fulfill. Our "it-could-be-our-last-chance" opportunity to make a meaningful and important contribution to the generations that will follow us, will present itself each time we sit down to talk with our loved ones. Oh, they won't know or even sense it, but we'll know we've got a job to do. God wants us to influence their lives, and He'll be there guiding us to move forward saying, *"Give them honesty, integrity, and the capacity for unconditional love."*

The role of a parent will be our labor of love. We will know that in reality our biggest responsibility on earth will be to hang onto and fulfill our role as parents. Oh, we'll acknowledge (often reluctantly) that we need more help from our children, and we'll give them more duties to support our everyday independence. Grocery shopping, bill paying, filling pill containers, and arranging transportation will eventually be delegated to those we love so much. However, the role of being a parent will be the role that we will keep. After all, the role of a parent is our responsibility forever.

When my dad died, I was forty-seven, my mom was sixty-seven, and my grandmother was eighty-seven. This was the first time that I really understood how strong and powerful the role of a parent really is.

None of us were ready for Dad to die, that's for sure, but the pain my mom experienced was totally devastating. It was horrible to know how much she was hurting and to realize that her pain would continue day and night for a very long time. To some degree we knew her pain would really last forever.

My brothers and sisters, and Ray and I, as well as all my siblings' spouses, tried so hard to swallow our own grief to do our best to comfort Mom. It was January and after five days of helplessly watching my father die in an Orlando, Florida, hospital, we took him home to Indiana to say, "Goodbye."

My grandmother was living in the nursing home near my mom's Indiana home by then and was really quite frail. The weather was nasty cold in northern Indiana and my mom told me to talk to my grandmother and to tell Grandma that Mom wanted her to stay at the nursing home. Mom was afraid that my grandma just couldn't handle the cold to come to the funeral. "Tell Grandma I really want her not to come," my mom insisted. And just as my mother had asked me to do, I went straight to the nursing home to see my grandmother and to explain that Mom really wanted her not to come. It was below zero and the wind-chill factor was just way too much for Grandma to tolerate.

Grandma listened intently as I explained my mother's wishes. She protested as I knew she would, but then in the end, I really thought she understood and that I had convinced her to stay inside protected from the ice and snow and chilling cold.

Then bright and early the next morning, when all of us were gathered at Mom's house and getting ready to go to the funeral home, the phone rang and it was the nursing home with my grandmother on the line. Grandma simply said, "Karen, tell me one more time why your mother is telling me not to come." I explained once more about the cold and snow and ice and that Mom was really afraid that it would be just too much for her. After just a moment of silence, Grandma responded in a tone that made me know her message was one that I must obey. She said, "That reason is just not good enough."

Without any further argument, I said, "OK Grandma, I'll call Aunt Lil and ask her to come and pick you up and bring you."

Grandma came to the funeral home bundled up in coat and scarf and boots, arriving just a few minutes after the doors opened and a long line of family and friends began to pour in. I will never forget seeing her frail, little frame passing through the crowded vestibule. With her cane in one hand, providing a little necessary balance, and the other hand gently grasping the top of each pew as she walked, she moved quickly and directly down the center aisle.

Everyone separated a bit as they saw her coming to let her pass by. She determinedly pressed on with tearful eyes focused on her destination. Without seeming to notice all the people and without speaking a word to anyone, she walked straight ahead to where she knew her daughter would be seated.

As she took her place in that very first pew next to Mom and gently put her arm around her daughter's shoulder, Mom leaned in towards Grandma, tilting her head to Grandma's shoulder. Grandma knew she was where she belonged as a parent, and I knew right then that no matter how old we are, we will always be parents.

The principles of life define who we are and, with God's help, we will pass them on, leaving them to our children and our children's children. Honesty, integrity, and unconditional love—God gave them to us at birth and asks us to value them as treasures of life and then to someday leave them as our legacy for future generations.

Who are the people that we love so much? How can we act to expand our own capacity and teach others to be honest and live with integrity? How can we truly give love unconditionally? Deep within our souls, we find the answer to our challenge. We find it in our everyday life and we find it in prayer. With God's help, we find it and know that in some small way the world will be a better place because we did.

Chapter 22

God's Kingdom

Everybody Wants to Go to Heaven but Nobody Wants to Die

As we fast-forward our thinking to the end of our retirement years, we realize that the success of our retirement and, actually, the success of our entire lives is based on the story that we tell of the life that we have lived. Hopefully, we can look back and quietly claim our victories and humbly recognize the contributions we have made to the world we have lived in for so many years. Oh yes, we could have done so much more. We could have been a better person, kinder, and more considerate. Yet, now in reality, we know that this is not the time to dwell on our failures or to waste energy on things we *could have* or *should have* done differently.

We need to focus on today and look to tomorrow, lingering in the reality of each day and striving to enjoy the little pleasures of life that so many other people don't even notice. We thank God for everything He has given us and thank Him for the opportunity to live our lives.

Looking ahead and anticipating heaven, we wonder with simple human curiosity, eager to know more about eternity. Our thoughts often go to loved ones who have passed away before us, and we enjoy fantasizing about the pleasure of reuniting with them in a place we call heaven. We are calm and confident, not anxious or afraid. Death will not come as a big surprise for we have lived a long life. No, it won't be a surprise for us, and it won't be a surprise for our loved ones either. Our prayer is for a happy death—peaceful without suffering.

Our thoughts go to those who will be left behind, and we pray that God will comfort them when we are gone. Close to our hearts are memories of those we have loved so much, and of the sorrow we felt when they left us to move on to God's kingdom.

We will remember our parents and grandparents and what their old age was like. Mental notes are made comparing ourselves to our loved ones who have already gone on to heaven, especially those who lived long lives.

God's kingdom is a mysterious place that we can't begin to imagine or even to dream about. On one hand, we are fearful of the unknown and, on the other hand, we are ready. Our faith is strong and our confidence in God reassuring.

Prayers become more like heartfelt conversations with our very best friends, only better and more meaningful. God knows us better than we know ourselves. He talks to us in a new way or, perhaps, we just listen more and really hear His words. Our relationship with Him is less formal now as we begin to feel more and more comfortable in His presence.

We have enjoyed our retirement years and are experiencing the aging process contemplating our own death and anticipating eternal life. Although we'll never really know what heaven will be like, our confidence will grow that God's kingdom will be wonderful just as He promised.

Someday soon we believe that we will see those who have gone before us. We will reunite with loved ones that have been missed so much. Drawn towards God, we'll develop a deep desire to know Him better. More curious and less afraid—we'll be somewhat afraid of dying but, yet, at the same time, curiously drawn to it. And, gradually over our own personal span of time, we'll become more and more curious and less and less afraid.

Our relationship with our loved ones—especially our children—will become stronger and better. Worried about how others will handle our death, we will want to continue to be needed but, at the same time, want to know that everyone will be OK without us.

Dear God, please let me go quickly without pain and let my family feel comfort in knowing that I didn't suffer.

Dear God, please bless my children and grandchildren. Give them a good life and keep them safe.

Dear God, please bring my children close to you; teach them to know you and to love you.

Chapter 23

Hope, Faith, and Encouragement

Hope tugs at our heart strings and at our soul repeatedly, revitalizing our existence and drawing us toward our destiny. Faith propels our spirit and gives birth to each morning and to every new opportunity. Encouragement is the driving force that creates the actions we take and empower others to take to help us each become the best person we can be.

Yes hope, faith, and encouragement somehow come to us as a package neatly wrapped around our lives promising us happiness and a sense of fulfillment. With hope, faith, and encouragement, life is wonderful beyond any imagination of its potential.

Yet, in the reality of our lives as we have lived them thus far, we have all known despair and the anguish of the absence of hope. We've experienced the pain of suffering and of loss and felt sorry for ourselves and for others. We have wallowed in our own self-pity, doubted our faith, and challenged God for the deaf ear He seemed to have turned towards us and our needs. We have been discouraged and afraid.

From the dungeons of despair to the galaxy of hope, from the darkness of doubt to the brilliance of faith, from the discouragement of discontentment to the encouragement of empowering satisfaction—that's the destiny we must choose. That's the path we know we want to take. That's our past tense that now encompasses our present tense and will someday turn to all our future tomorrows.

Oh, there must be hundreds and thousands of people who came before us who travelled the path of hope, faith, and encouragement. They are our role models and inspiration. They are our brothers and sisters, aunts and uncles, mothers and fathers, children and grandchildren, spouses and friends. They are the people who have touched our lives. We remember their courage, their confidence, and their love.

We choose to join their forces and embrace their quality of life and try to emulate their character. Humbly we look within ourselves to find the hope, faith, and encouragement we need to succeed.

I am inspired by the simple Christian prayer, the *Prayer of Saint Francis*. Distributed by Cardinal Spellman during World War II, quoted by Margaret Thatcher when she became prime minister, prayed daily by Mother Teresa, and sung by hundreds of thousands as the hymn version, *Make Me a Channel of Your Peace;* this beautiful prayer speaks to our hearts.

The Prayer of Saint Francis

Lord, make me an instrument of Thy peace;

Where there is hatred, let me sow love;

Where there is injury, pardon;

Where there is doubt, faith;

Where there is despair, hope;

Where there is darkness, light;

And where there is sadness, joy.

Oh Divine Master,

Grant that I may not so much seek to be consoled as to console;

To be understood, as to understand;

To be loved, as to love;

For it is in giving that we receive,

It is in pardoning that we are pardoned,

And it is in dying that we are born to Eternal Life.

Amen.

Chapter 24
The Meaning of Success!

Thank you for travelling this wonderful, retirement journey with me. It's been an inspiring adventure. We've had endless opportunities to explore life and been given so many chances to choose our own destination.

And now, our journey continues with more opportunities to succeed and to reap the rewards of our own successful living. As we travel through retirement time, we develop a clear image of what retirement success is really like. With every new opportunity, we gain experience. Insight is gained to better understand and appreciate our chosen destiny. We even begin to realize and to accept the outcome of the life events that were given to us without discussion. In some cases, we find good in what others might consider life's misfortunes and acknowledge that some things were just meant to be.

Successful retirement life is an extension of successful living that comes from our own maturity and our personal desire to be happy and fulfilled. We continue to enhance our own quality of life by reaching out to help others discover their own potential.

Choosing to be doers, not observers, we make contributions to improve the world around us. Reaching out, we touch the lives of others we love.

We learn to love those whose lives we thought we'd never begin to understand. Comprehending the actions of others or approving of their choices is not the prerequisite to unconditional love. We learn to love unconditionally (at least most of the time) and will continue trying to perfect our skill.

Questioning others' motives comes to a stop, and we let go of the grudges we've held in the past—even those carried for a very long time. It feels so good to just move on and forget about the hurt and the sorrow of yesterday and embrace the peace and joy of today. Eager to take a quick peek into tomorrow, we anticipate with excitement all the new opportunities that will surely be waiting for us. We enjoy life and celebrate successful living.

We continue to work hard to be the person we always wanted to be. Old habits die hard and it's not always easy to set ourselves free. Yet bad habits are just bad habits that became automatic out of repetition. They don't really represent who we are now, nor do they exemplify how we want to be in the future—no more growling and complaining; no more judging or condemning.

Retirement success is something found, not by measuring and comparing all of life's circumstances, but by learning to look for the good in others and realizing that when we look for it, we'll find it.

The world we live in is a wonderful place. Our life is filled with opportunity. The success that we experience is a success that is uniquely our own. We live and love, give generously, and realize we have so much to be thankful for. We celebrate the true meaning of success.

Appendix

Retirement Success Stories

Here are excerpts from stories of some special people who took time to share their thoughts regarding the list of topics introduced in Chapter Three (page 15, *Define Your Priorities)* and in the Appendix on page 93.

Joetta, Caldwell, Montana:

Joetta celebrated her seventieth birthday this year and has enjoyed successful retirement life for more than seventeen years now. She has been, and continues to be, an inspiration to me and to all who seek retirement success. Joetta raised four children and retired from a successful career as a corporate trainer and manager at age fifty-three. She gives insight and inspiration to all who seek to live a fulfilling and rewarding retirement life. Here are her thoughts:

"Following the far too early death of my first husband, I had a small nagging feeling I needed to do and see more."

*"The decision to retire was not so much **from** but **going forward**."*

"My job gave me the opportunity to travel and in many ways taught me to be independent."

"My first year I wanted to see new things, I wanted to see the Grand Canyon and much more."

"My children were grown. The baby was ready to go to college. I felt at the time that all four of my children would grow more independent with my moving on. (I had not been a mother who could say no.)"

"After the death of my first husband, I met and later married a man (who was) fifteen years older than me who loved to travel. He brought me to Montana and there I found a completely new life."

"Financial Security was provided from my first husband plus I learned to need less to live."

"During my life I have visited every state with the exception of Hawaii."

(Leisure Time) *". . . is both all the time and never enough time for."*

(Day-to-Day Living) *"Of course there is some routine but I try not to get too set with routine or maybe 'set in my ways.' I feel it is important for me to be flexible in most of what I do. I have learned that life is far too short and I don't want to miss anything if I can help it."*

(Family) *"Children of course come first and fill such a large part of my heart."*

"I have found through two husbands and one 'almost' husband that extended families are very important. One of the sweetest things said to me when my second husband died was from his oldest sister. She said 'I'm not sure what my brother did to get you, but he did and then he gave you to us.'"

"As we grow older, families grow also and become more precious. I am one of eight children and our annual get together is powerful."

"Following the death of my second husband I worked part time as an aid for Home Health Care Services. I found this so rewarding and very interesting. My patients were in their homes, often remote ranches. They were able to have some control of their lives in their homes and able to tell stories about their lives. When I look back at this and other parts of my life I see how important service and care giving is to me."

(Spirituality) *"I can be with fellow believers or sitting on a big rock near our mountain home talking to God—wherever, that is our foundation. I know I can have many people in my heart but I must have that one corner saved for Jesus."*

Richard and Patti, Oakton, Virginia:

Richard is seventy-two and Patti is sixty-five and they have been retired for more than twelve years. Richard retired from a marketing executive career and Patti from a writer/proposal development position. Richard dabbled in consultancy work for a short time after retiring. Now Richard and Patti are very active and they enjoy reaching out to others. Patti lists her "retirement occupation" as *Writer, Researcher, Traveler, Mentor, Student, and Consultant to inner city ministry and family elders.*

Patti tells their story:

*"Retirement was sort of 'given' to me, in a sad way. My mother was slowly dying of terminal cancer. I took my company's family emergency medical leave of 12 weeks, I think it was. The time came to an end, and Mom was still lingering. I was told to report back to work or I would be fired. In a panic I phoned my financial manger, who gently asked me, 'Do you really **LIKE** this job?' 'Are you **KIDDING**?' was my reply. 'It's making me **SICK!!**' My job was **VERY** stressful, with **LONG** hours, endless government deadlines, with very little 'thanks' after the fact. I suffered many stress-related illnesses over the years. Plus, I lost my husband 3 years earlier (1992) and had a lot of difficulty dealing with that. My financial guy then said, 'Well, you know, you don't **HAVE** to work.' The thought had never occurred to me. I was speechless. He explained that **IF I** could live frugally, I could squeak by on my widow's pension, plus use some of my investments if need be. I ended up tendering a letter of **RESIGNATION** to my company, and I never looked back. It's been a **GREAT** 12 years of freedom to pick and choose how I want to live my life. I feel truly blessed."*

*"My first year involved simply 'finding myself.' I was under a great deal of emotional stress. At least I got to spend more precious time with my mother before she passed away. As my internist told me, 'You only get to do this once.' It made me painfully aware of making the best choices for me at any given time. Eventually, I was able to review what my strengths were, where my passions lay, and where I wanted to spend my time. I was not only 'redefining' myself as a young widow; I was looking for my own special 'niche' in the world of retirement. It's **OUT** there. You just have to find it!!"*

*"We are very blessed to have a relatively stable degree of financial security, having planned well in the early years. This cannot be over stressed. Young people today have really never experienced national hardship, such as our parents did in World War II and the Great Depression. They have never **REALLY** been 'without' and expect that things will always **BE** that way. They rarely have any classes in school to prepare them for wise financial planning, and many of them become bogged down in mountains of debt before graduating college, becoming slaves to their creditors for years to come. While there is really no such thing as 'security,' it is incumbent upon each of us to be responsible for our own retirement years. As the old adage goes, 'Fail to plan. Plan to fail.' And the younger we begin, the better; but it's never too late!"*

*"There are never enough hours in the day, it seems, to do all the many things we would like. We have decided to make a 'priority list' of all the places we would **REALLY** like to see before we get 'too old and crotchety' to navigate! Each year, we try to take one 'big trip' on our list, and then we usually have other smaller, side trips to do research, visit family, and so on."*

"We are fairly active in our church and try to give back to our community through various church related outreaches. One involves inner city, at-risk youth, where we have served over 10 years. We have also identified ways to give back while we live in our winter home, such as Habitat for Humanity."

"(OLLI: One of the best kept secrets we have discovered is the Lifelong Learning Institute for seniors. Many local universities are affiliated with it. The one in our area is called OLLI (Osher Lifelong Learning Institute). For a reasonable amount of money (paid annually), you can take all KINDS of classes, usually in your own neighborhood. Offerings include anything from Bridge, to Painting, to French Conversation, to Philosophy, to The Psychology of Aging, and countless more. Our program also offers many great field trips (for a small fee) and something called 'Fall for the Book'—a lecture series given by several famous authors each year.)"

"Amazing stuff!! Plus, you find new friends who enjoy the same interests you do. I was thrilled to discover that the woman teaching French was the daughter of my beloved French teacher from high school. We almost cried when we first saw each other!! Her mother has passed away, and we love to reminisce about what a wonderful lady she was. We even dig out some of her old 'lessons' and use them in class."

"Before we married, we went through premarital counseling. We were told to write a 'Marriage Mission,' defining the goals we hoped to accomplish by becoming husband and wife. We also identified our core values as mature adults—very eye-opening, and a good exercise for anyone. It really helped us focus on how we wanted to spend our leisure time."

"My husband is a longtime golfer and truly loves "the game." I am a book worm—a lifelong bibliophile. I also thoroughly enjoy watching sports on TV. Because we have some very diverse hobbies, we make time to sit and talk every day, beginning the morning with a wonderful devotional. We read the Bible out loud to each other and pray for our families. This, more than anything has kept our marriage very anchored.'

"We try to maintain a balance of time together and time pursuing our own passions. I am reminded of a line from one of my favorite poet philosophers, Khalil Gibran: 'Let there be spaces in your togetherness. The old oak tree grows not in the cypress tree's shadow.' We all need our 'space' which makes the times together all the sweeter."

"Family is absolutely 'huge' for us. Part of our marriage mission was to 'pour Christ' into the little ones, to make sure the torch of our faith is passed down to the next generation. We want that 'circle' to be unbroken one day when our work here is finished."

"We were both raised by parents who survived the Great Depression and WW II. We feel blessed not to have voracious material appetites, and we try not to spend what money we have foolishly. We are both very big on the left hand knowing what the right hand is doing"

"We both really feel we are living our dreams today. Being a cancer survivor, and both of us having lost our spouses, we try to live each day to the fullest, firmly anchored in the present moment."

"We express ourselves through prayer and worship; listening to our kids, creating great vacation, [sic] pursuing research goals (genealogy); decorating our home; occasional gardening; reaching out to the community."

(Growing old together/growing old alone) *"Planning for when you need to give up your home, turn in your driver's license, and move into the 'home' is not a fun thing to think about, but looking ahead is important. We have put together what we call the Vital Records Book. It contains all of the information our children will need when we are incapacitated. We have listed our lawyers, doctors, banks, insurance companies, where the will is located, where all the cemetery lots are, and so on. I have also labeled china, vases, and other family memorabilia for identification 'one day.' The whole idea is making things as easy as possible when hard times arrive."*

"Getting old together? We are doing THAT right now, moment by moment. We both notice at times our memories are not quite as sharp as they once were, our eyesight is a little dimmer, our hearing slightly impaired, so we try to be sensible and take things a little easier that we did in our younger years. No climbing on high ladders. No lifting heavy furniture. No jumping over fences."

(Words of Wisdom) *"There is no time like the present. With a grateful heart, get out there and find your 'niche'!! There are tremendous ways to learn new things, express who you are, and to 'serve' others as well. In so doing, you will find true, inner peace and joy. Giving is ultimately its own reward."*

"Think outside the box. This is your chance to really be flexible and do some things you always dreamed of doing. Try volunteering in an area that sounds interesting. You

may discover something new about yourself. Expect great things, but be willing to change your course. You're not 'locked in' now. "

"Expand your horizons, Carpe Diem!! Today is the first day of the rest of your life. It doesn't matter how you think you 'failed' in the past. This is your opportunity to let loose, have fun, and go seize your destiny. There is a big world to discover out there. Go enjoy it!"

Don and Barbara, Galien, Michigan:

Don and Barb just retired last month. Barb is 55 years old and Don is 59 ½. Both have worked in the transportation field. Don, a semi driver, delivered oxygen to health care facilities. Barb supervised transportation for her school system. Barb made the decision to retire for the couple's insurance benefits available through her retirement after thirty years in the school system. Barb continues driving a school bus in a part-time capacity as she is easing into retirement life. Barb shares her thoughts about retirement:

"Making the decision to retire was a very hard decision that took a lot of thought and many sleepless nights. You question your decision and think to yourself I could and probably should work for several more years for the money. I don't think you ever feel as if there is enough money."

(Someday dreams) *"Somewhere warm in the winters for awhile, maybe starting in the next few years. . ."*

"I would like to volunteer to mentor a child or at a homeless shelter. I believe the homeless shelter would help you to appreciate what you have and quit wishing for more."

"My purpose in life is to be a good person, wife, mother, friend, grandmother and to know that somewhere along the way I made a difference in someone's life."

"Growing old doesn't scare me, but I never want to grow old alone. It's sure nice to know that I don't have to wake up alone and that I have someone to share my hopes, dreams and fears with."

"Life is short, you just never know how short. My advice would be to retire while you have your health and are young enough to do what you want to do with whatever time you have left."

Chapter 3—Define Your Priorities

What is really important to you? What is really important to your spouse? I suggest every couple and every individual contemplating retirement sits down and writes a retirement plan that defines your desired retirement life. Complete the following worksheet to help you define your priorities. You may want to continue your reflections on a separate sheet of paper. Don't limit yourself to a few lines.

A List of Topics to Reflect On

1. Make the decision to retire (assess your personal desire to retire; consider your current work satisfaction, family situation, lifestyle needs, and finances):

2. Your first year of retirement (What do you plan to do? How will you explore your future?)

3. Financial security and lifestyle satisfaction (What kind of lifestyle is important to you? What steps will you take to secure your financial future?):

4. Travel and activities:

5. Together and individual interests (Consider your interests, your spouse's interests, and those of your family. What kinds of things do you and your spouse enjoy doing together? What things do you enjoy doing alone?):

6. Leisure time:

7. Day-to-day living:

8. Family (Consider family needs and relationships and how they change when you are retired.):

9. Money (money management, your budget—what you will do to feel financially secure during retirement):

10. Someday dreams (What are your dreams and how will you fulfill them?):

11. Self-expression (consider self-worth, personal identity):

12. Volunteering (Is volunteer work important to you? How does that fit into your retirement plan?):

13. Part-time employment (How do you feel about working part-time during retirement? What might you do?):

14. Spirituality:

15. Purpose in life:

16. Health and fitness:

17. Chronic illness, disease, and physical limitations:

18. Words of wisdom (What thoughts might you share with others who are already retired or planning on retiring soon?):

19. Growing old together/growing old alone:

20. Advice for others who are retiring (What would you encourage others to think about in relationship to retirement?):

Chapter 8—Who Am I Now That I Have Retired?

Complete the sentences in any order or add your own beginning to the sentence. Start writing and keep writing. Let your thoughts flow freely.

1. I am:

2. I know I am:

3. I have the capacity to:

4. I sometimes:

5. I can:

6. I need to:

7. I want to:

8. It's important to me to:

9. Others see me as:

10. I am happiest and most fulfilled when I am:

Chapter 9—Consider the Need for Retirement Credentials

Template for Resume

Following the format of the template, create your resume.

(name)
(address)
(city, state, zip)
(phone)
(e-mail)

(Your Descriptive Title)

Write a paragraph that explains what you do and the services you provide.

Projects Include:

(Make a list.)

Professional and Business Resources:

(List any resources you would like to use.)

Background:

(Describe your background and experience.)

Professional History:

(List employment history.)

Accomplishments:

(Give a few examples of things you have accomplished.)

Business Acknowledgements:

(List quotes from others that give credit for your work or recognition for your accomplishments.)

Chapter 10—Write an Annual Anniversary Retirement Message

The objective of writing an annual retirement message is to create a summary of the year that will tell your own personal story of how you are living your retirement life. Your summary should be rather brief and to the point so it truly reflects the key messages you want to keep for posterity and to share with your family in years to come.

To help you look back on your past year and remember the events that you want to highlight, I suggest you consider the following points:

1. On a separate sheet of paper, make a list of everything you did this past year. You may find it helpful to review your calendar to jar your memory. (Note: If you have already been retired for a number of years, then just start by summarizing your retirement experiences so far.)

As you make your list, go back to the retirement priorities list that you created earlier. This will help you remember the things that happened as well as consider the significance of each event.

Remember the first year was the year of exploration. As you write your summary, ask yourself, How did you do at exploring and self-discovery? Share your thoughts.

Your message will someday be your legacy—write with an optimistic attitude and include your personal insight on how you will approach the upcoming year. What are your plans? Your goals? Your intentions?

2. Write your Annual Retirement Message as a brief story (one or two pages) that explains the significance of the key points from your list. Write your message on the following pages or store your document in a journal or a computer file so you, as well as your heirs, can look back and enjoy your memories.

(Repeat this process every year and celebrate your own retirement success.)

First Year of Retirement Message

Second Year of Retirement Message

Third Year of Retirement Message